CHINA

from Manchu
to Mao (1699-1976)

CH

from Manchu
to Mao (1699-1976)

John R. Roberson

ILLUSTRATED WITH PHOTOGRAPHS,
PRINTS AND MAP

ATHENEUM   New York   1980

The author wishes to thank Ross Tirrell for permission to use two quotes from Mao Zedung (pages 153 and 173) that originally appear in his book *The Future of China After Mao,* published by Delacorte.

PICTURE CREDITS:

New York Public Library Collection: pages 16, 17, 20, 32, 35, 58, 66
Prints Division, The New York Public Library, Astor, Lenox and Tilden
    Foundations: pages 6-7
Museum of the American China Trade: pages 12-13, 51
National Archives: pages 47, 48, 54, 55, 78, 84, 95, 101, 109, 111, 115,
    123, 139,
New China Magazine: pages 89, 128, 136, 158, 164, 177
U.S.–China Peoples Friendship Association: pages 145, 147, 178-79
U.S. Information Service: pages 166, 168-69, 171

LIBRARY OF CONGRESS CATALOGING IN PUBLICATION DATA

Roberson, John R.   China from Manchu to Mao.

    Bibliography: p. 181
    Includes index.

    SUMMARY: A history of China during the last three centuries, from the
time Western nations began to play an important part in Chinese affairs.
    1. China—History—Ch'ing dynasty, 1644-1912—Juvenile literature. 2. China
—History—Republic, 1912-1949—Juvenile literature. 3. China—History—
1949-1976—Juvenile literature. [1. China—History—Ch'ing dynasty, 1644-1912.
2. China—History—Republic, 1912-1949. 3. China—History—1949-1976]
I. Title.
DS754.R7   951   79-22269
ISBN 0-689-30758-6

To three generations of
ROBERSONS
who love China

Contents

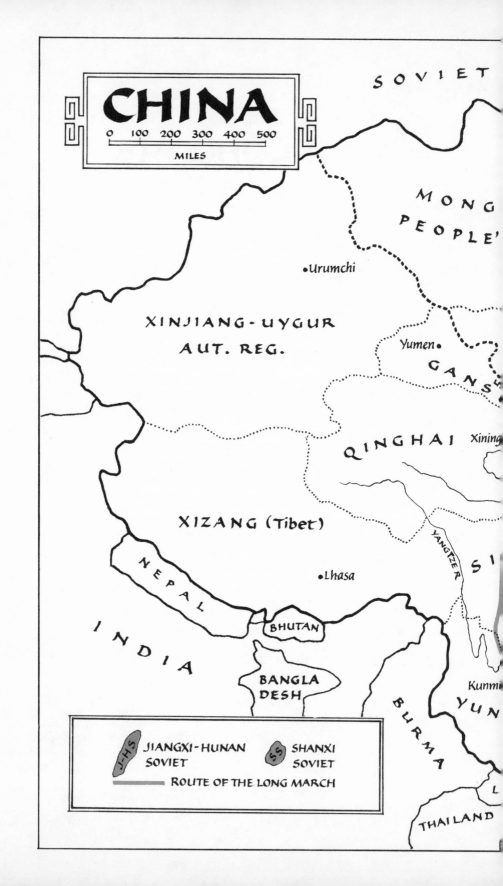

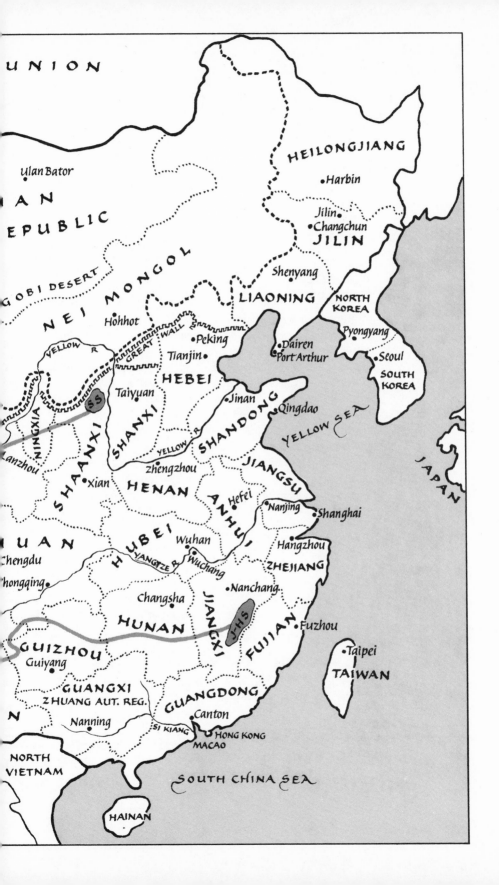

The author has kept the number of Chinese names in his text to a minimum. This glossary will serve as a key to identification and approximate pronunciation of names essential to the history covered. Spellings long established in English— Peking, Canton, Nanking, Yangtze, Manchuria, Confucius, Chiang Kaishek, Sun Yatsen—have been retained. All other names are given in the system for writing Chinese sounds in the Roman alphabet adopted early in 1979 by most magazines and newspapers in the United States. It is the Chinese government's official system, called pinyin. To help students in consulting materials that use the older, Wade-Giles system of "romanization" of Chinese, this Glossary gives the Wade-Giles forms in parentheses. All names in the index are also cross-referenced for the two systems.

PEOPLE

Ci Xi (Tz'u-hsi) *TSOO shee*
   Empress Dowager, the power behind the throne in China 1861–1908

Chiang Kaishek (Chiang K'ai-shek) *JAHNG ky-SHECK*
   Leader of the Nationalist Party 1928–1975, President of the Republic of China

Chinese Names

Confucius (K'ung Fu-tzu)
Philosopher and teacher, lived 551–479 B.C.

Deng Xiaoping (Teng Hsiao-p'ing) *DUNG she-OW-PING*
Vice-Premier of the People's Republic of China, 1974–

Hong Xiuchuan (Hung Hsiu-ch'uan) *HOONG sio-CHWAHN*
Leader of the Taiping Rebellion of 1851–1864

Hua Guofeng (Hua Kuo-feng) *WAH GWO-fung*
Premier of the People's Republic of China 1976–

Jiang Qing (Chiang Ch'ing) *JAHNG CHING*
Wife of Mao Zedong and member of the influential "Gang of Four" in the Political Bureau

Kang Xi (K'ang Hsi) *KAHNG shee*
Manchu emperor, reigned 1661–1722

Lin Biao (Lin Piao) *LINN be-OW*
General who commanded Chinese Communist armies in the Korean War 1950–1953

xii · CHINESE NAMES

Liu Shaoqi (Liu Shao-ch'i) *li-O SHOW-chee*
  Chairman of the People's Republic 1959–1968, advocate of the Economist Line in government policy

Mao Zedong (Mao Tse-tung) *MOW TSAY-doong*
  Founder of the People's Republic of China, Chairman of the Chinese Communist Party 1935–1976

Qian Long (Ch'ien Lung) *CHIN LOONG*
  Manchu emperor, reigned 1736–1796

Sun Yatsen (Sun I-hsien) *SUN yat-SENN*
  Statesman and revolutionary leader, founded the Republic of China in 1911

Zhou Enlai (Chou En-lai) *JO in-LY*
  Premier of the People's Republic 1949–1976, and its most effective diplomat

Zhu De (Chu Teh) *JU DUH*
  Top commander of Communist armies in the fight against the Nationalists

PLACES

Canton (Kuang-chou)
  The major port of south China

Chongqing (Ch'ung-ch'ing) *CHOONG CHING*
  City in central China on the Yangtze River, capital of the nation during World War II

Manchuria
  Region of northeastern China, including the provinces of Heilongjiang, Jilin and Liaoning

Nanking (Nan-ching)
>City in eastern China, capital of the nation at various times, most recently 1928–1937 and 1946–1949

Peking (Pei-ching)
>City in north China, the nation's capital during most of the last 1000 years

Shanghai (Shang-hai)
>China's largest city, at the mouth of the Yangtze River

Tianjin (T'ien-tsin) *TIN-JIN*
>Transportation and trade center for Peking

Yan'an (Yen-an) *YUN-AHN*
>City in north central China, a Communist stronghold during the revolution

Yangtze (Yang-tze) *YAHNG-zee*
>China's longest river, flowing across the center of the country

n April 26, 1699, the emperor of China made a bow-and-arrow shot so spectacular that it is still remembered today. The emperor was Kang Xi, one of China's best in all ways; the occasion was an imperial visit to the city of Hangzhou, on a tour of the southern provinces of the empire. Since archery on horseback was his favorite sport, an archery competition was one of numerous entertainments scheduled during his stay.

That day the best archers in the Imperial Bodyguard demonstrated their skill. Then it was the emperor's turn. First he rode across the width of the range and shot as his horse passed in front of the target. His arrow hit the mark. Then he turned to a more difficult exercise—shooting as his horse galloped down the range straight toward the target. Just as he was about to release his arrow, for some reason his horse swerved to the left. The crowd of spectators was horrified. Both the emperor's hands were occupied with the bow and arrow. Would he be thrown from his horse?

Kang Xi stayed in the saddle. He quickly changed his grip on the bow, took new aim, and hit the target squarely again. A shiver of relief and admiration ran through the

ONE

Barbarians from the West

crowd. Among those present were the emperor's mother, seven of his sons, numerous ministers of state, royal secretaries, court historians, and officials of the province and city. All these dignitaries were seated in exact order of their rank in the imperial hierarchy.

Outside the archery range, ordinary citizens jostled each other for a glimpse of the emperor. Word of his feat quickly spread to them. Kang Xi was always solicitous of their welfare, and they loved him for it. When he went on tour, the people decorated the route he traveled with arches covered with silk brocade and poles decorated with brightly colored streamers, ribbons, and bows. At night, Chinese paper lanterns, some in the shapes of fish or dragons, shone along the way.

Perhaps somewhere on the very outskirts of the crowd were a few foreigners—Roman Catholic scholar-priests who had come to China from faraway Europe. As non-Chinese, they were considered the lowest ranking people present. Their activities and travel were closely restricted. But in Kang Xi's glorious sixty-year reign, the influence of the foreigners in China was to grow and grow.

Kang Xi was the first emperor to recognize that there

熙　康　祖　聖　清

The Manchu Emperor Kang Xi began to rule China when
he was fourteen. He spent long hours at his desk, writing
brush in hand, issuing decrees for the benefit of his people
and became one of the best rulers the country ever had.

were certain things mighty China could learn from Europe, and he was the first to sign a treaty with a Western nation (the 1689 Treaty of Nerchinsk with Russia). From his time on, the dominant theme in China's history is the impact of Western nations on the world's oldest continuous civilization.

Still, on that triumphant spring day in 1699, no one would have believed that two centuries later Europeans would control the Chinese capital for a few months. Or that the empress of China would hide in a lowly peasant's cart to escape from the city.

Kang Xi had been emperor of China since 1661, since he was eight years old. At first a council of ministers ruled for him, but by the time he was fourteen he was considered wise enough to guide his empire himself. Confidence in his ability was completely justified.

The young ruler was strong, well built, and somewhat taller than others his age. But people noticed most his eyes—large, bright eyes that lighted up his face and gave an indication of the intelligence behind them. Strength and courage enabled him to lead his imperial armies time after time to victory over invaders on China's borders and over rebels at home. Intelligence and hard work enabled him to give his country good, stable government, and with it prosperity.

More than a dozen times he toured his empire, for as he said, "One should see everything for oneself." He stopped to chat with many people en route, ranging from the poorest peasant, farming land belonging to someone else, through landowners, scholars, provincial officials and

MARCHE ORDINAIRE DE L'EMPEREUR DE LA CHINE

Dedié à Monseigneur
Ministre d'État Controleur Général des Finances

When the emperor toured the country, the people decorated
his route with arches covered in silk brocade and with poles
flying brightly colored streamers.

LORSQU'IL PASSE DANS LA VILLE DE PÉKING.

Charles Alexandre de Calonne,

Commandeur et Grand Trésorier des Ordres du Roi.

Par son très-humble et très-Obéissant Serviteur Helman.

governors. He asked about crops and local problems, and sometimes joined fishermen fishing. He even talked with the European missionaries.

Kang Xi was particularly concerned with China's vast system of canals. Through a thousand years the Chinese had developed these canals to provide irrigation for their crops, flood control, and water transportation. The chief highway of the empire, in fact, was the Grand Canal stretching from Tianjin in the north to Hangzhou, 850 miles to the south.

The emperor was very fond of maps, and on tour would sometimes spread a map in front of him and point out details of the canal system to his officials. He wanted very much to have a good map of his entire empire, whose borders he had expanded farther than any emperor before him. One of the Europeans in Peking, the Jesuit scholar Ferdinand de Verbiest, had drawn a map of the world that particularly impressed the emperor. As a result, in 1708 Kang Xi commissioned the Jesuit missionaries to map his empire. The task took nearly ten years, as the mapmakers studied the best European and Chinese maps of that day, and actually surveyed the land in some areas themselves.

When the new map was finished, it showed China with approximately the same boundaries it has today. In the semitropical south, a fertile land of terraced rice fields carefully tended and irrigated, China bordered on what is now Vietnam. Inland, the boundary was marked by the snowy Himalayan Mountains, the world's highest range, separating China from Burma and India. Tibet, astride the Himalaya, would soon be added to the empire by Kang Xi. Farther north was Outer Mongolia, bordering on Russia. (Because of the terrain and the scattered population, the exact boundaries in the west and northwest remained inexact.) From Mongolia, east to the Pacific, China's northern boundary was marked by the Amur River, under the terms of the treaty Kang Xi had signed with the Russians. On the north bank was Siberia; on the south bank, Manchuria, the home of the Manchu tribe that had conquered all China and made Kang Xi's father emperor in 1644.

Kang Xi ruled all this vast territory by force when he had to. But he much preferred to earn the allegiance of his people by ruling well. He saw to it that promotions were awarded on the basis of knowledge and merit, and rooted out corruption at all levels of government. He lived modestly himself, and repeatedly reduced the taxes on his people. He encouraged education and the arts, and assembled a group of scholars to compile a great encyclopedia to make available in one place the accumulated wisdom of the centuries.

In all these ways Kang Xi sought to fulfill the Chinese view of the ideal society—a view set forth more than two thousand years before by China's most revered philosopher, Confucius.

In the view of Confucius, the structure of a nation was shaped like a pyramid. The emperor was at the peak, and the people formed the broad base. The whole structure was held together by "right relationships" between its parts, between those below and those above. Good sons and daughters revered their parents, in a close-knit family. The head of the family respected the landowning gentry in the village, who in turn owed allegiance to the village and provincial officials. And so the pyramid was built, right up to its tip, the emperor.

In the Confucian ideal, force played no part in these relationships. The emperor would rule as long as he was good and wise, and his heirs would succeed him. If the emperor did not measure up, the whole structure would fall apart, and China would seek a new emperor worthy to found a new dynasty.

Kang Xi was determined to measure up. And China under his rule did seem to enjoy "right relationships," all through society.

There was one problem. The Confucian view of the world made no adequate provision for non-Chinese. It assumed that China was the center of the world, the only civilized nation, and that all other people were simple barbarians who would gladly pay tribute to the Chinese emperor in return for the opportunity to sample a bit of Chinese culture. By Kang Xi's time, this assumption, held for thousands of years, was being challenged.

The challengers came from Europe—a continent the Chinese were only vaguely aware of, located somewhere bordering what they called the Great Western Ocean (the Atlantic). Some seemed civilized enough. The European priests wanted to learn about Chinese culture, and talk about astronomy and mathematics and religion—particularly about their own religion, Christianity. Various emperors before Kang Xi had allowed them to maintain a sort of school in Peking, and Kang Xi conferred a great honor by allowing them to instruct him personally in mathematics.

But other Europeans were rough sea captains and sailors, who knew nothing of the etiquette of accepted behavior in China. They came determined to establish trade. For Europeans had sampled Chinese silks and tea, and a great demand for such luxuries had developed. Kings and merchants both saw prospects of enormous profits from commerce with rich China, with its millions of inhabitants.

The Chinese were glad enough to sell their products,

as long as they were paid in good silver money. But they thought it wise to keep close control over these foreign merchants. So they limited their trading activities to only one port, Canton, on China's south coast, the port farthest away from the court and capital at Peking. This cautious policy Kang Xi continued.

The reign of Kang Xi lasted for sixty years. In 1722, at the age of sixty-eight, the emperor caught a fatal cold while pursuing his archery—hunting on horseback on the wild Steppes of Mongolia.

Kang Xi's son succeeded him for a comparatively brief reign of fourteen years. He was followed by his son, Qian Long, who achieved another sixty-year reign. From the beginning of Kang Xi's rule to the end of Qian Long's was a span of 134 years. The Manchu Dynasty, called in Chinese the Qing, or "bright," lasted until 1911, in all, 267 years. But after the standard of excellence established by the first Manchu emperors, especially by Kang Xi, it was downhill all the way.

Zealous Chinese today maintain that European meddling was responsible for the decline. Ardent Westerners maintain that the West's chief goal was to benefit China by bringing her into contact with the rest of the world. There is some truth in both positions, though neither gives the whole story.

Whatever their motives, Westerners became more and more active in China during the reign of Qian Long. The

FOLLOWING PAGES: *In the eighteenth century, Westerners eager to buy the fine teas and luxurious silks of China were allowed to build warehouses near Canton, identified by their national flags. But the Chinese resisted all efforts to trade at other ports.*

China trade grew enormously. In the eighteenth century, England and Holland were the chief seafaring nations of Europe. Then, their ships competed with new rivals, the Yankee sea captains from New England. Clipper ships built in America were the swiftest on the seas, and each year they loaded the first Chinese tea harvest on board and raced to London. This first tea of the season commanded premium prices among Englishmen, some of whom would drink twenty cups in an evening.

One port in so vast a country was hardly adequate for the potential trade, and the merchants constantly sought to have China's policy changed. In 1793, King George III of England, still smarting from the loss of his American colonies, sent a delegation to Qian Long to ask, as one ruler to another, that additional ports be opened to English merchants. The emperor's reply was patient but firm:

> *Yesterday your ambassador petitioned my ministers to memorialize me regarding your trade with China, but his proposal is not consistent with our dynastic usage and cannot be entertained. . . . Our Celestial Empire possesses all things in prolific abundance and lacks no product within its own borders. There was, therefore, no need to import the manufactures of outside barbarians in exchange for our own produce. . . . Nevertheless, I do not forget the lonely remoteness of your island, cut off from the world by intervening wastes of sea, nor do I overlook your excusable ignorance of the usages of Our Celestial Empire. I have consequently commanded my ministers to enlighten your ambassador on the subject, and have ordered the departure of the mission. . . .*

Subsequent delegations had even less success.

Qian Long's claim that his empire possessed all things and lacked for nothing was very nearly true. China enjoyed a long period of peace, disturbed by only minor rebellions and border skirmishes. The arts flourished. Literature reached new heights, and Chinese kilns produced some of the most beautiful porcelain ever seen.

It was a Golden Age. And yet it produced its own problems. The population increased rapidly, creating the need for increased production of food. But China was already farming all of her land that was suitable for agriculture. In years when crops were poor, thousands starved.

Part of each year's crop, in both good years and bad, went to feed the army. The soldiers grew fat and lazy, and their discipline lax. Even the elite Manchu regiments, so proud and powerful when their forebears conquered China in 1644, grew soft. The Manchus, both military and civilian, had maintained their separate identity in all the years since the conquest, wearing their hair loose while requiring the Chinese to braid theirs in a pigtail called a queue. Manchus could marry only other Manchus. And yet the longer they ruled in China, the more they appreciated Chinese ways, and the more like Chinese they became.

Qian Long himself grew soft, and fond of the easy life. The end of his reign was far different from that of his grandfather. Kang Xi had kept vigorous and alert to the very end, riding his horses, studying his mathematics, traveling and keeping a close eye on all his empire. He died at sixty-eight. Qian Long reigned to the age of eighty-five. First he grew weary of the duties of office, and then so senile that he did not know what was happening in the government. The Confucian doctrine proved all too true, that the ruler at the top of the pyramid of society sets the tone of the whole.

The Emperor Qian Long (reigned 1736–1796) gave China a Golden Age of magnificent art and literature. But he entrusted too many decisions to ministers who were corrupt. Government became weak, and the people suffered.

More and more Qian Long entrusted government decisions to his ministers of state, and chose as ministers his favorite people, regardless of their abilities. Some of these

favorites used their power to accumulate wealth for themselves. One notorious official, before he was finally exposed,
put together a private fortune equivalent to a billion dollars
in today's money. Graft diverted public money to private
pockets, with the result that taxes rose and yet public works
suffered—including the irrigation system necessary to grow
food. Tariffs were collected on foreign trade at Canton, but
the Western merchants complained that the rates were not

*In 1793 Emperor Qian Long received an ambassador (far
right) sent by King George III of England to propose an
expansion of trade between the two countries. China had no
need, said the emperor, "to import the products of outside
barbarians."*

set in an orderly way, but by the whim, or greed, of the tariff officials.

Worst of all, Qian Long neglected the civil service system that had given China such good government. When this system operated properly, all positions were filled on the basis of difficult competitive examinations. That ensured that the best men ran the vast empire, and government officials, or "mandarins," were highly respected for their learning. But as corruption spread, it became possible to buy a passing grade on the examinations. There was even a known price scale for admittance to various ranks in government.

In 1796, the sixtieth year of his reign, Qian Long stepped down from the throne and made his son, Jia Qing, emperor in his place. The official explanation was that he did not want to rule longer than his illustrious grandfather. The new emperor had grown up amid the increasing corruption of the court, and showed little desire to set things straight. He ruled for twenty-four years, during which conditions grew worse and worse.

The decline of good government in China provided new opportunities for the Western merchants. Since the volume of merchandise that could pass through the one port of Canton was small, and the ocean freight route around the tip of Africa to Europe was long and expensive, the traders naturally sought to deal in goods that would command the highest prices. Silk and tea were the Chinese products most in demand in Europe. But Europe produced no goods the Chinese wanted in exchange, as Qian Long had pointed out to George III.

All nations know that trade is a two-way street. Europe could not continue to buy from China, if China did not buy from Europe. Casting around for a solution to the eighteenth-century balance of payments problem, the merchants hit upon a miserable solution. They taught the Chinese to smoke the drug opium, derived from certain species of poppy that grow in Asia. China grew these poppies in small quantities to make medicine from the seeds, but in neighboring India, where the opium smoking habit was long established, poppy production was enormous. The European merchants saw that they could sell Indian opium to Chinese addicts. As the supply of the drug in China increased, so did the number of addicts, and the trade snowballed.

The Chinese government issued strict edicts prohibiting the sale or smoking of opium. But the very nature of the drug trade makes its control difficult. Smuggling developed. The stakes were high, the desire for the narcotic intense, and the effects of its use destructive to a sense of morality. Corrupt officials, some of them addicts themselves, closed their eyes to the smuggling, or shared in the profits.

By the time Jia Qing was succeeded as emperor by Dao Guang in 1820, the balance of payments situation was completely reversed. Exports through Canton were insufficient to pay for all the opium coming in, and the Chinese had to pay the difference in silver. The emperor now had a double reason to stop the opium trade: to protect his subjects' health, and to protect his empire's finances. Finally, in 1839, he appointed an imperial commissioner to go to Canton and abolish the opium trade once and for all.

Since India was at that time under English rule, English merchants had the most ready access to the opium supply. The showdown came, therefore, between the imperial commissioner, whose name was Lin Ze-xu, and the English superintendent of trade in Canton, Sir Charles

In 1841 the British navy bombarded Canton, as a result of
drastic Chinese efforts to stop foreigners from selling opium
in the city. This "Opium War" forced China to open four
additional ports to Western trade.

Elliott. Commissioner Lin, a week after he arrived, simply seized the foreign warehouses in the city, and held the merchants as hostages. Then he suggested to Elliott that he persuade his countrymen to surrender all the opium in their possession, without compensation. That came to 20,283 chests, more than 2,000 tons of opium. Elliott had no choice but to comply.

The commissioner's next act surprised everyone in the cynical city, so accustomed to corruption and political pressures. He destroyed all the opium, publicly, on a beach near the city. "The process took twenty-three days," he reported. "Even the foreigners came to watch and . . . lavishly praised the commissioner's integrity."

The story did not have a happy ending. Commissioner Lin made other demands of the merchants. The British government retaliated by demanding payment to the merchants for the opium destroyed, and sent warships to back up the demand. War followed—a war whose underlying purpose was to open China to all sorts of foreign trade. The British called it the "Trade War," but, not surprisingly, the Chinese had another name, which has stuck in the history books—"The Opium War."

The emperor's forces were no match for the British fleet, which captured and held for a time the ports of Shanghai and Nanking, as well as Canton. The Chinese for centuries had regarded their nation as the mightiest in the world. They could hardly believe such defeats at the hands of the "barbarians." But by 1842, they were ready to yield to British demands.

The principal demand was for the opening of five ports to British trade—the old goal, achieved at last. In addition, the British demanded and got outright possession of the island of Hong Kong, near Canton.

The Chinese agreed to pay for the opium Commissioner Lin had destroyed. And the British government promised to end the smuggling of opium—a promise that proved impossible to keep.

In the next two years, China signed additional treaties with Britain, France, and the United States, with additional provisions for trade. Tariff rates were fixed. The foreign merchants were granted tracts of land, called "concessions," to live on in the open ports. These concessions were to be little bits of foreign soil in China, where the foreigners would not be subject to Chinese law. If they were accused of crimes, they would be tried under the laws of their home country. In legal language, this arrangement gave the concessions "extraterritorial status." This provision troubled diplomatic relations for the next hundred years.

The treaty with the United States contained an additional provision that proved even more of a burden to China. It promised for the future that if China granted further privileges to the citizens of any nation, those same privileges would be automatically extended to American citizens also. The provision was known as the "Most Favored Nation Clause"—insurance that no other nation would be more favored than the United States. The same clause was inserted in treaties won by other countries, thus multiplying the effects of whatever diplomatic defeats China suffered in the years ahead.

Those defeats were to be numerous, as foreign pressure on the proud Middle Kingdom grew stronger and stronger.

hina's first treaty with the United States was signed in 1844. That was exactly 200 years after the fierce warriors from Manchuria captured Peking and established the Manchu Dynasty. No dynasty had ever kept its strength forever, and the Manchus were showing signs of weakness. The 1844 treaty, and the similar ones with Britain, France, and Russia, had been forced upon the emperor, whose armies were unable to oppose foreign invasion. In domestic affairs, the government was full of injustice, graft and corruption.

Thoughtful Chinese were well aware that their nation now fell far short of the ideal state described by Confucius. Perhaps the time had come for the Manchus to be replaced. And so in the nineteenth century various leaders led rebellions against the dynasty.

The most important of these rebel leaders failed to overthrow the Manchus, but the ideas he planted in the minds of the nation were so powerful that they still have influence today. He was born in 1814 in the province of Guangdong, not far from Canton. His family name was Hong.

TWO

Three Attempts at Reform

Young Hong demonstrated at an early age that he had a brilliant mind, and his family and the people of his village encouraged him to study for the civil service examinations that would admit him to a career in government. He passed the preliminary tests, but when he went to Canton, the provincial capital, for the all-important final examinations, he was competing with a thousand applicants for only a dozen posts. Although he took the examinations, given annually, several times, he was never among the successful few, perhaps because he did not have the money to bribe the chief examiner.

Between examination attempts, Hong taught school in his village and continued studying to learn more and more about the Chinese classics. The examination questions were limited to the ancient learning of China, on the theory that an official well versed in the traditional wisdom would be able to make his own practical applications. But Hong gained practical knowledge too in Canton, for it was the principal gateway for all the Western influence that was flooding into China. There he saw the Western merchants, and talked with the Christian missionaries. One missionary gave him a Chinese translation of parts of the Bible, which

Hong scanned and put away to read at some later date. He heard of secret societies meeting in the city to work for the overthrow of the Manchu Dynasty and the return of a strictly Chinese emperor to the throne. And Hong saw the corruption of that dynasty at close hand, in the examination system and in the opium trade.

After taking the examinations in 1837, Hong, age twenty-three, was exhausted in mind and body. He fell sick and had to be carried home to his village. For four days he was delirious, with a high fever. When he came to himself again, he told of a wonderful dream he had had. Hong had probably never heard of Joan of Arc, but Westerners who learned of his dream were inevitably reminded of the peasant girl's vision in which the Virgin Mary commanded her to lead an army to save France. In Hong's dream, an old man with a golden beard appeared to him and told him he should call himself by a new given name, Xiuchuan, meaning "accomplished and perfected." He should take the title Younger Brother of Christ. And he should lead an army to save China from oppression. To guide him, the old man gave Hong a book.

After he had this dream, Hong's whole personality changed. He stood erect, and walked with a firm step, so that he actually seemed taller than before. His piercing eyes and confident way of speaking attracted attention. He began to take an active interest in local and national politics. And he wore his hair loose, in open defiance of the Manchu order that all Chinese wear pigtails.

For six years, Hong brooded about his dream, and the command he had been given. In 1843, he took the civil service examination for the last time. That year a cousin, looking through Hong's books, found the volume of excerpts from the Bible given by the Christian missionary.

He brought it to Hong's attention and Hong read it carefully this time. Here, he believed, was an explanation of his dream. The old man was the God of the Bible. Since he had called Hong the Younger Brother of Christ, Hong was God's son. And the book in the dream was this very book he was reading. Hong went back to Canton the next year to learn more about Christianity, and studied for a short time with an American missionary.

Hong gradually formed in his mind his own religion—a version of Christianity with Chinese elements added, the whole modified by what he considered a personal revelation from God to him. He began to travel about the province of Guangdong and neighboring Guangxi, preaching and winning thousands of converts to a band he called the "God Worshippers." Some sincerely believed his religious message. Some hoped he would free them from government oppression. And some, ambitious military men, saw in his band a rallying point for a force large enough to further their own careers.

Hong worked with all the energy of an inspired fanatic. His criticism of the Manchu Dynasty became sharper and sharper. But the imperial officials ignored the God Worshippers, as just another of many small groups that were constantly agitating for various changes.

In 1850, thirteen years after Hong had his dream, the Emperor Dao Guang died. His successor, Xian Feng, was a man of weak character. The time seemed ripe for an uprising. The leaders of the God Worshippers called all their followers to assemble in a mountain village, and more than 10,000 came. The authorities, alarmed at last, sent troops to invade the village, but Hong's followers fought their way out and escaped into the rugged mountains. Now they were committed to open rebellion.

On January 11, 1851, Hong issued a formal proclamation phrased in language reminiscent of Moses' return from Mount Sinai. It read, in part:

Our Heavenly Prince has received the Divine Commission to exterminate the Manchus—to exterminate all idolators generally, and to possess the Empire as its True Sovereign. It and everything in it is his, its mountains and rivers, its broad lands and public treasuries; you and all that you have, your family, males and females from yourself to your youngest child, and your property from your patrimonial estates to the bracelet on your infant's arm. We command the services of all, and we take everything. All who resist us are rebels and idolatrous demons, and we kill them without sparing; but whoever acknowledges our Heavenly Prince and exerts himself in our service shall have full reward—due honor and station in the armies and Court of the Heavenly Dynasty.

Hong then proclaimed himself "Heavenly King." The kingdom he was to rule over, once he had won it in battle, he called "The Heavenly Kingdom of Great Peace— *Taiping Tianguo*." Hong's campaign became known as the Taiping Rebellion, the Great Peace Rebellion. Estimates of those killed in the fourteen years of this "Great Peace" war run as high as twenty million, or five percent of the population of China at that time.

In the next three years Hong was enormously successful. As he marched north out of the mountains, thousands more joined his army. He proposed a detailed program for righting the wrongs of the people, which today's rulers point out as the forerunner of Chinese Communism. It included common ownership of all property, with land classified according to its fertility and distributed equally. Women were regarded as equals, and so were the foreigners who had taught Hong Christianity. The systems of taxes and governmental administration were to be reformed: opium, tobacco, alcohol and prostitution were all prohibited.

In 1853, Hong captured the city of Nanking, the ancient capital of China, and proclaimed it capital once again. His armies pushed on north toward Peking. Reports to the young emperor from those provincial officials whose duty it was to maintain order understated the seriousness of the threat. When Taiping victories could be hidden no longer, the emperor found his armies in no shape to do battle.

That year the imperial throne was saved not by valorous defense but by the distances of China. The rebels could win battle after battle in the countryside. But they did not have the organization, the transport, the supply services, in short the logistical support to lay siege to the walled city of Peking, six hundred miles from their headquarters in Nanking. Forays reached as close as Tianjin, eighty miles short of the goal, but did not occupy the country permanently in the north.

The emperor, on the other hand, proved no more capable of launching a successful effort to recapture Nanking. For eleven years China was divided, its southern half ruled by the rebels.

During the long stalemate neither side was able to build up enough strength to defeat the other. Hong's splendid program of reform, announced with such assurance, needed skilled administrators to put it into practice. But his ideology repelled the bureaucrats trained in the old

Confucian order who had grown rich through corruption. They wanted no part of the Heavenly Kingdom of Great Peace. And indeed many of Hong's most ardent followers pursued personal advancement more than reform for the entire country. His leaders disagreed and quarreled, and Hong was unable to find in himself or in his visions the statesmanship needed to govern successfully.

In the first years of the rebellion, the Western nations dealing with China avoided taking sides. Hong's reform program called the Europeans "fellow Christians" and "equals." Not all the Europeans returned the compliment. Some felt that Hong's version of Christianity was blasphemous. Others, less interested in theology than in trade, favored the Manchus in the struggle because they had at last granted some of the privileges the Europeans had been seeking for so long. Still others hoped that the Taipings, if they ruled all China, might be easier to deal with than the corrupt Manchu Dynasty.

Western indecision came to an end in 1860, when Hong's troops approached Shanghai, hoping to seize arms and ammunition stored there. This port at the mouth of the Yangtze River had grown rapidly since it was opened to trade, and was destined by its location to become the major European trading center in China. The foreign residents there had recruited a small troop of mercenary soldiers for their defense, a force soon given the grandiose title of "The Ever Victorious Army." This troop repelled the Taiping attack on Shanghai, and Western nations sent reinforcements to fight the rebels.

In 1863, a young major in the British Royal Engineers was given command of the Ever Victorious Army. His name was Charles George Gordon. He made the army's name a reality and it in turn gave him a name that stayed with him through a brilliant career on three continents: Chinese Gordon.

Gordon quickly shaped the small band into an effective fighting force, and led them out of Shanghai to capture town after town from the Taipings. Chinese provincial officials had also formed local militia to fight the Taipings when they saw they could expect little protection from the imperial armies. The Western nations now supplied these militia with arms and with instructors to teach modern warfare. The Taipings, attacked by Gordon and by the Chinese militia, lost control of the Yangtze River valley bit by bit. By the spring of 1864, Hong Xiuchuan, Heavenly King, saw that his dream was ended. In June of that year he died in his capital at Nanking. According to one story he committed suicide by swallowing a handful of gold coins. Nanking fell, and the Taiping Rebellion was over.

While China was weakened by this disastrous civil war, the Western powers gained more and more control over her affairs. Foreign trade had grown enormously as a result of the opening of the five ports in 1842. Customs duties collected on this trade proved a rich source of revenue for the government. The Chinese and the Western nations together established a maritime custom service for all the ports. An Englishman, Sir Robert Hart, enormously able and strictly honest, served as Imperial Inspector General of Customs for forty-four years. He became the most respected Westerner in China—respected by both the Chinese and the Europeans. Yet his presence in China was an admission that the Manchu Dynasty could not carry out a government function as basic as tax collection.

The foreign merchants constantly sought to have more of China opened to trade, including the inland ports along the mighty Yangtze, the chief route to the interior. The

emperor refused. In late 1856, the British and French re-solved to obtain additional rights by force, using a shipping incident as a pretext for war.

The British occupied Canton in 1857 and in 1860 a combined British and French force took the northern port city of Tianjin and fought overland to Peking. On the way, they looted and burned one of China's great architectural treasures, a collection of some two hundred buildings known as the emperor's summer palace. This action was intended as retaliation for Chinese violation of a truce, and the killing of twenty prisoners. But the Chinese re-member it still as an unwarranted and barbarous act.

In 1860, the emperor was forced to sign treaties that opened ten more ports, including four on the Yangtze, to trading ships and to foreign warships on patrol duty. The treaties also allowed foreigners to live and trade in the interior of China, including in Peking itself. And they granted Westerners the right to carry on missionary ac-tivities in the interior.

Christian missionaries, both Roman Catholic and Protestant, had been active before that in those parts of China where they were allowed. One of the most effective ways to reach the Chinese, they found, was to establish hospitals. Western medicine proved more effective than the ancient Chinese variety, a further demonstration that not all foreigners were ignorant barbarians. The missionaries also set up schools to teach the people to read and write, as

In 1860 British forces waded ashore near Tianjin in North China. Joined by French troops, they fought overland to Peking and forced the emperor to allow foreigners to live and trade there and in many other cities.

well as to understand Christianity and a little bit about the world outside China. One of their students traveled to the United States, where he was graduated from Yale University. Others followed.

In arms, in government administration, in science, the Westerners were proving themselves the equals, or better, of the proud Chinese. China's strength and prestige at the signing of the treaties in 1860 seemed at a new low.

The next year a new ruler appeared on the scene—the strongest the nation had in all the nineteenth-century. This ruler was clever, ruthless, strong-willed—and a woman.

In 1861, the Emperor Xian Feng died. His son and heir was only five years old. So the child's mother was designated one of two regents to rule for him. Supposedly the regency would last only until the child was old enough to rule for himself. But this regent managed to remain the power behind the throne for forty-seven years.

In that time she held various titles and was known by various names—some respectful, some not. She is most often remembered as Ci Xi, Empress Dowager, her title as mother of the emperor.

In 1851, when this remarkable woman was seventeen, she had been one of a group of girls presented at the palace so that the Emperor Xian Feng could choose additional concubines to give him pleasure. She was chosen a concubine of the fifth rank—in ordered China, there was a hierarchy for everything. Her beauty and her spirit soon caused her to become one of the emperor's favorites, and when she gave him the son he had been longing for, she became the most important woman in the country.

The girl who became the Empress Dowager Ci Xi was chosen for the imperial court when she was seventeen. She gave the emperor the heir he had been longing for and ruled as the power behind the throne in China for forty-seven years.

Women in China, as elsewhere at that time, were rarely educated. They were trained in domestic skills and graces, but scholarship and public affairs were for men only. The young mother was ambitious. She had a will strong as a tigress. But she knew the emperor was weak and she had to protect herself and her son from the palace intrigues of a court without scruples. She must learn the arts—and tricks —of government that interested the emperor so little.

Tutors and books were not lacking in the palace, so she learned to read and write the difficult Chinese language, skills that eluded even ninety-nine per cent of the male population. After that she read many books, though without the overall direction that would have made her really educated. In after years it amazed those who dealt with her that she knew so much about the world and understood so little.

The tricks of the court could not be learned in books, but Ci Xi had a native shrewdness, and an amazing capability of judging people. She also had an absolute singleness of purpose that drove her forward, and kept from her mind any considerations of mercy. The members of the court who suffered mysterious deaths—deaths that benefited Ci Xi and her son—cannot be counted accurately. It seemed that the life expectancy of her foes could be reckoned in months; Ci Xi herself lived to be seventy-four.

The Empress Dowager once summed up her career to a trusted member of the court, the Princess Der Ling:

> Do you know, I have often thought that I am the most clever woman who ever lived, and others cannot compare with me. Although I have heard much about Queen Victoria and read a part of her life, which someone has translated into Chinese, still I don't think

*her life was half so interesting and eventful as mine.
My life is not finished yet and no one knows what is
going to happen in the future. I may surprise the
foreigners someday with something extraordinary and
do something quite contrary to anything I have yet
done. England is one of the great powers of the world,
but this has not been brought about by Queen
Victoria's absolute rule. She had the able men of
Parliament behind her at all times and of course they
discussed everything until the best result was obtained,
then she would sign the necessary documents and
really had nothing to say about the policy of the
country.*

*Now look at me. I have four hundred million people,
all dependent on my judgment. Although I have the
Grand Council to consult with, they only look after
the different appointments, but anything of an
important nature I must decide myself. What does the
emperor know? I have been very successful so far.*

The organization of the executive branch of the government in China in 1861 can be compared roughly with
that in the United States, substituting a hereditary emperor
for our elected president. Orders of our president are carried out by the Cabinet, made up of the heads of the Departments of Agriculture, Commerce, and so on. Each state
in the nation has its governor. In China, orders of the
regent, Ci Xi, issued in the name of the emperor, were
carried out by the Grand Council, made up of the heads of
the Board of Agriculture, the Board of Rites and so on.
And each province had its governor.

By coincidence, 1861 saw both China and the United

States engaged in civil war, with rival governments proclaimed in the south of each country. In China, the imperial government never managed to regain its absolute
control of the entire nation, in either an administrative or
a military sense.

As regent in such tumultuous times, Ci Xi needed
good advice. She chose three men to trust, and her choices
were excellent. One was Prince Gong, the brother of the
late emperor, whom she made head of the Grand Council.
The second was the provincial governor who organized the
Chinese army that eventually defeated the Taiping rebels.
His name was Zeng Guofan. And the third was Zeng's
young assistant, Li Hongzhang. Of course, seeking good
advice is one thing and following it is another. But at least
in the beinning Ci Xi listened more often than not.

All three of these advisers believed that China could
regain her old strength by a two-pronged program: reviving
ancient virtues and studying Western science, especially
armaments. The Confucian state, successful for so many
centuries, would then be restored to strength and adequately
defended. For them, the possibility that the basic Confucian
structure might be incompatible with Western ways was
unthinkable.

Their goal they called the Restoration of the Confucian
State, and their means they called "self-strengthening." To
restore the Confucian state to its former glory, Ci Xi's advisers cleaned up the corruption in the civil service examination system, recruited honest and able officials, and encouraged farming (the base of the Confucian pyramid) by
lowering land taxes, opening additional land to cultivation,
and repairing the irrigation system. And they exhorted the
nation to follow the ancient ideals of right conduct and
right relationships.

To facilitate learning from the West, a special department was established in the government to deal with foreign affairs. Prince Gong himself headed this Chinese version of foreign office. No longer were foreign ambassadors treated as tribute-bearers from barbarous states, or refused a hearing at Peking and sent back to the provinces to deal with lesser officials. Now the diplomats were assigned a section of Peking where they could establish embassies or legations and live with their families and staff. This "foreign quarter" soon developed into a little island of Western life in the city.

To strengthen China's military defense, the advisers established arsenals to make Western style weapons. They sent more students to study abroad. And they set up offices to translate Western books, especially scientific books, into Chinese.

There were still many leaders in China who objected to all this foreign influence and they were quick to point out that hopes of a limited Westernization were false. Ships and guns require steel, and steel requires coal, and coal requires railroads to bring it from the mines. All those requirements mean capital must be invested, and investments must be managed. In short, Western arms could only be produced by Western industrial organization. But the Confucian learning offered no guidance for industrialists and capitalists, and the Confucian pyramid-shaped society of farmers, landowners, mandarins and court ministers hampered industrial expansion. Each industrial enterprise had to have a government official as a sponsor before it could be launched, which meant it was enmeshed in bureaucracy from its very beginning. Project after project began and soon failed.

After a decade, the drive for self-strengthening bogged

down. And other advisers had won the ear of Ci Xi—men less interested in what was good for China than in what was good for them. They flattered the empress dowager, and she was glad to listen to their flattery. The longer she maintained her position, the more confidence she gained in her own judgment. And the more she enjoyed her power.

In 1875, Ci Xi's son, the emperor, was nineteen years old, and ready to rule for himself. He had married, and his wife was expecting a child. But that year the young emperor developed a mysterious sickness and died. Three months later his wife also died—of grief, according to the official explanation. Some suspect both deaths were actually murders, although the truth concerning them is still not known.

Since the emperor died without an heir, the Grand Council had to designate his successor. Ci Xi, who had the support of the army, forced the council to choose her infant nephew as emperor, and make her regent again. Her power was assured for at least another fourteen years. During that time the government came to be dominated more and more by her favorites and members of her family, regardless of their abilities. The overall interests of China were subordinated more than ever to private ambitions.

The advocates of self-strengthening despaired that it would ever come about. Obstacles were everywhere. Farmers were afraid of such modern inventions as the steam locomotive. Government officials in the lower ranks feared that the introduction of Western ideas would cost them their jobs. And the great numbers of useless hangers-on at court naturally urged Ci Xi to keep things the way they were and reject foreign ways. All these groups opposed change, and made the work of reform more and more difficult. Money from taxes that should have gone for public works paid instead for luxuries at court. The most notorious case concerned money allocated to build a modern navy.

The empress dowager managed to divert the money to one of her pet projects, the rebuilding of the summer palace destroyed by the French and English in 1860.

The Western nations saw in China's new dilemma a new opportunity. If China wanted steel mills and ship-yards and coal mines and railroads and telegraph lines, Westerners would be happy to build them—for a price. The rewards of investment in a nation with so many potential customers seemed enormous. Soon all the trading nations of Europe were scrambling for the lion's share of the profits, and each was asking the imperial government to assign exclusive rights for the industrial development of certain areas of the country. As the Chinese expressed it, the Europeans viewed China as a great melon, which they wanted to carve up among them. It was the age of imperialism. The Europeans had already divided up the whole continent of Africa. Closer to China, the French had achieved control of Vietnam and the British ruled in Burma —two areas that had formerly paid tribute to the Chinese emperor. And one nation in Asia, Japan, had learned West-ern lessons so quickly that it had achieved a high degree of industrialization, built a modern navy, and annexed Okinawa and the other Ryukyu Islands as the first step toward building a colonial empire in Asia. Next, the Jap-anese turned their attention to the part of the Asiatic mainland nearest to them, the peninsula of Korea.

Korea had given allegiance to China for centuries, and China resolved to oppose with force Japanese expansion there. China declared war, she said, to save Korea from "the dust of bondage." Japan declared war, she said, to end China's interference in Korea's domestic affairs.

The war was decided on the sea, where China's navy was defeated in the first battle. That meant China could not prevent Japan from pouring troops in. The Chinese soldiers who reached Korea fought doggedly, but could not drive out the Japanese. Ci Xi's government sought peace. The Treaty of Shimonoseki of April, 1895, ceded to Japan the Pescadores Islands and Formosa (Taiwan), and proclaimed the end of Korea's allegiance to China. By 1910, Japan had gained complete domination of Korea.

Defeat by the Japanese, a people the Chinese had long scorned, was much more humiliating than defeats by the Europeans. But the pain of defeat was not without its benefits. It made Chinese all over the country realize that what the reformers had been saying was true. The imperial government was in need of a basic overhaul if it was to escape the fate of so many previous dynasties.

In the government, the only influential advocate of self-strengthening left was Li Hongzhang, who was in his seventies. In 1895, discussing reform, he said, "Affairs in my country have been so confined by tradition that I could not accomplish what I desired. . . . Now, in the twinkling of an eye, ten years have gone by, and everything is still the same."

Outside the court circle, the leader of reform thought was a scholar, Kang Yuwei, who had studied in Japan and written several books on how Japan and Russia had modernized their societies. Kang organized in China a Society for the Study of National Strengthening.

National strength was almost entirely lacking. The European nations viewed China's defeat by Japan as a signal that the power of the empire was ended. They pressed more vigorously for permission to develop railroads and industry, and Ci Xi had no choice but to yield. Britain,

France and Germany were each granted "spheres of influence"—geographic areas of China where they had exclusive rights to economic development.

In 1898, the Emperor Guang Xu was twenty-three, but his aunt, Ci Xi, was still really in command at court. That year the young emperor resolved to assert his authority. With the help of Kang Yuwei, and the Society for the Study of National Strengthening, he attempted to right some of the wrongs in his country. He received Kang at court, and ordered him to submit his proposals for nationwide reform.

During the summer of 1898—a period known as the "Hundred Days of Reform"—the Emperor issued edicts to implement Kang's proposals. He ordered modernization of education, government administration, commerce and the military services, and he declared an end to many useless offices at court.

A strong, active emperor had no place, however, in the plans of the empress dowager. On September 16, with the help of two of the most powerful generals in China, Ci Xi staged a *coup d'etat*. She seized control of the government, arrested most of the reform leaders, and put the emperor under a sort of house arrest that lasted until he died ten years later. Kang fled to Japan.

In the second half of the nineteenth century, three major attempts to change the Chinese state had failed: the Taiping Rebellion, the self-strengthening movement of the 1860s, and now reform backed by the emperor himself.

Ci Xi, for all her shrewdness, was not able to understand that changes in the regime were necessary and inevitable. By thwarting the orderly reform proposed in 1898, she postponed those changes for a short time. Two years later, demands for change took a more violent form.

fter the Empress Dowager Ci Xi overcame by force the leaders of the Hundred Days of Reform of 1898, conservatives rallied behind her. But the conditions that the reformers sought to improve were still present all over China. Dissatisfaction with the Manchu Dynasty increased. So did hostility to the foreigners who had wrested so many privileges from that dynasty.

Since the reform efforts of the intellectuals had failed, many Chinese advocated change by violence. Thousands joined a secret society named the Yi He Duan, meaning literally the Society of the Righteous Fists, but translated by the Europeans as "the Boxers." The Boxers' program was simple: end foreign influence in China.

The Society used an unusual recruiting device—the promise that initiation into its ranks made members invulnerable to bullets. And indeed they held public demonstrations that proved to the satisfaction of many that the promise was true.

In north China, where the Boxers were most numerous, foreign influence meant chiefly the Christian missionaries

THREE

Throw Out
the Foreign Devils

sent out by Catholic and Protestant churches in Europe and America. In 1899, the Boxers began raiding the mission stations, burning the buildings and sometimes killing the missionaries, but more often killing numbers of their Chinese converts, whom the Boxers regarded as traitors. As the killings increased, the Westerners left their missions and sought protection in the legations in Peking. Each new group arriving brought word that the Boxers were growing in strength, and were coming closer and closer to the capital. No one knew what they might do when they reached the city wall. In early June the Western diplomats addressed a number of petitions to the Chinese government asking protection for their fellow citizens. They also sent requests for help to the small military bases that various nations maintained, by right of treaty, at Tianjin, eighty miles east of Peking.

Ci Xi's ministers assured the diplomats of full protection, but did little. Perhaps the government lacked the military strength to suppress such widespread violence. Or perhaps the empress dowager hoped to play the Boxers against the foreigners, to save her dynasty. Tension grew.

On June 13, 1900, the German minister to China, Baron Klemens von Ketteler, was walking on Legation Street in the diplomatic quarter of Peking. The street was filled with the usual mixture of many Oriental and Western nationalities. But one Chinese in particular caught von Ketteler's attention, because of the scarlet sash and kerchief that he wore—the insignia of the Boxers. As he rode along in a small cart, the Boxer stroked a large knife on the sole of his shoe, as if to sharpen it. The ambassador may have believed this to be a threat and he raised his walking stick and began to beat the man, who fled. A younger Chinese in the cart was not so quick, and got a good mauling.

On June 19, the Chinese Foreign Office sent identical notes to the ambassadors of the eleven nations that maintained legations in Peking: Austria-Hungary, Belgium, France, Germany, Great Britain, Holland, Italy, Japan, Russia, Spain and the United States. The notes mentioned in vague terms the unrest in the countryside and proposed that for their own safety all the diplomatic personnel leave Peking the next day. The government promised a military escort to the bases at Tianjin.

The ambassadors met in the French legation to debate the proper response to these notes. Despite their polite language, they seemed to convey a simple ultimatum: Get out of China. The argument grew heated. An Australian journalist named Morrison told the ambassadors that if they voted to leave Peking, they would be "known forever as the wickedest, weakest and most pusillanimous cowards who ever lived." The diplomats decided to stall for time, and telegraph again to the Tianjin bases for help.

The following day, June 20, Baron von Ketteler set out in his sedan chair for the Imperial Court. On his way, he was met by a young lance corporal of the Chinese Army,

*In 1900, United States Marines fought their way through the
streets of Peking to rescue 1,700 Westerners as shown in this
painting by a Marine sergeant. Members of an anti-foreign
society called the "Boxers" had laid siege to the section of the
city where the legations were.*

who shot him at point-blank range. Von Ketteler's death
put an end to the diplomats' debate, for he was killed
not by an unruly rebel, wearing the insignia of the Boxers, but by a soldier wearing the uniform of a Peking
Banner Regiment—the Manchus' elite troops. It was now
clear that the only immediate protection available to the
1,700 foreigners in Peking was the strength of their own
right arms.

The legation guards totaled twenty officers and 389
men, with the British, the Russian and the American guards
the most numerous. With the help of the civilians, they
fortified the legation quarter as best they could, strengthening various buildings with sandbags against the expected
attacks. The defense was aided by a comparatively recent

invention, the sewing machine. The ladies of the legations set to work making sandbags from whatever cloth was available: satin curtains, monogrammed sheets, gorgeous brocades in blues, reds and yellows.

Preparations for the defense had scarcely begun at 4:00 P.M. on June 20, twenty-four hours after the ultimatums had been delivered to the ambassadors. On the hour, the Chinese attack began, centering on the Austrian legation, on the northeast corner of the quarter. The defenders briskly returned the fire. No one knew it then, but help was still fifty-five days away.

The relief force that saved the Westerners from the Boxer troops in 1900 was made up of many nationalities. Posing here are Australian, Austrian and Italian sailors; French, German and American infantrymen; a Japanese cavalryman; British gunners; Sikhs and Bengal Lancers from India.

During that time, Ci Xi's government continued to express concern for the welfare of the diplomats. Ci Xi herself sent them a wagonload of fresh fruit. Historians are still not sure what were the true intentions of the wily empress dowager. But when the first telegram for help arrived in Tianjin, the foreign military men there organized an international rescue force. They attacked the fortifications of Tianjin, which blocked their route to Peking. Ci Xi responded to that attack by declaring war on the eleven nations involved. "You cannot declare war on the whole world," cautioned her Minister of War, Rong Lu. But it nearly amounted to that.

In Peking the legation quarter defense lines held all through the sweltering month of July. Finally in August additional British troops arrived in Tianjin, and the rescue force, now totalling 20,000 men, set out for Peking. On August 14, they broke through the walls of the city and ended the siege of the legations.

That night the empress dowager announced to the court that she was going on "an autumnal tour of inspection" in the provinces, and fled from her capital disguised as a peasant, hidden in a tiny cart.

Ci Xi's escape from Peking was entirely successful. With her went her nephew the Emperor Guang Xu, and a few courtiers. They headed southwest from the city, stopping the first few nights with local officials, always in fear someone would betray them to the Europeans. But by the time they reached the city of Xi'an, 600 miles away, they realized that no one was pursuing.

In Peking the military men had carried out their order, "Relieve the legations." They left it up to the diplomats to try to arrange the peace. The Europeans and Americans wanted punishment for those responsible for the deaths of their fellow citizens, cash indemnities to make up for the expense of the rescue force, and after that the chance to go right on trading in China. Of the three objectives, they considered the third by far the most important. Surely the imperial government needed to be reformed. But if the Allies threw their support behind the Chinese leaders who had taken part in the Hundred Days of Reform, who could predict what effect reorganization would have on trade? The concessions won laboriously through so many years were privileges granted by a court dominated by Ci Xi. And the arrangements worked out in the ports were arrangements with her officials. Might a reform government repudiate treaties, replace officials—upset the whole overloaded applecart? No one really believed the court's claim that the Boxers killed in defiance of imperial wishes, and that the empress dowager was unable to control them. Nevertheless, once the Westerners decided that they preferred Ci Xi to the reformers, that claim provided a way to save face for both sides. In September, 1901, the Westerners signed a protocol with the imperial government, providing punishments for various named individuals, and additional concessions for trade.

In 1902, Ci Xi returned to Peking, with the emperor still her virtual captive. Many of the Europeans were delighted to see her, among them the men who had been granted the right to build a railroad from Peking south. They conceived the idea that it would calm the people's fear of the "fire wagons," as they called the steam locomotives, if the empress dowager should return in glory on a train. Accordingly, they outfitted a magnificent group of coaches in dynastic style, and invited Ci Xi to ride in them the last twenty miles of her journey. Ci Xi liked the coaches very well; when she saw the fire wagon that was to pull them, she nearly backed out. But home she came. The

The Emperor Guang Xu, nephew of Ci Xi, was never allowed any real power. His aunt kept him almost a captive in the palace grounds, where his amusements included a very regal form of sledding on a frozen lake.

emperor went back to his house arrest. It seemed as if nothing had changed.

It soon became evident that Ci Xi herself had changed a bit. If the Westerners were so strong, and the Chinese so weak that she could not be secure in Peking's Forbidden City, she realized at last that China must learn from the West. Six hundred cold, hungry miles had made a point where six hundred memorials to the throne had failed. A number of her chief advisers had died and been replaced by younger men, with younger ideas. In the next six years, then, from 1902 to 1908, Ci Xi established new schools to teach Western subjects, allowed more students to study abroad, abolished the classical examinations for civil service positions, and set up an army reorganization council to create a modern army for China. China was on the road to a modern society at last.

I n the first decade of the twentieth century, the reforms instituted by the empress dowager Ci Xi made progress, although slowly. She sent a mission abroad to study parliamentary government—she was much interested in Queen Victoria and her advisers. In 1906, she announced that such a government would be introduced in China, and in 1908, she set a date for it—1917. Perhaps it was only coincidence that in 1917 Ci Xi would have been eighty-two—the age at which Victoria died. At any rate, it seemed certain Ci Xi did not intend to take an active part in a constitutionally governed China.

Such progress was not enough for the more ardent reformers. One of the most ardent was a physician who practiced more politics than medicine, Dr. Sun Yatsen. Sun was born in 1866, attended Canton University and a British medical school in Hong Kong. In his travels he became acquainted with the prosperous Chinese communities that flourished in most of the world's major cities by this time, as a consequence of nineteenth-century trading activities. These "overseas Chinese," as they called them-

FOUR

The Struggle For a Republic

selves, might have lived away from China for many generations, but they still felt that they belonged to their "old home," some spot in China where their ancestors had lived. They took a lively interest in what was going on in China. In 1894, when Sun Yatsen was twenty-eight, he organized in Honolulu the China Renaissance Society—a society dedicated to overthrowing the Manchu Dynasty and restoring China to the glories of the past. It was a theme as old as dynasties, but Sun was among the first to propound it among the overseas Chinese, and solicit financial support from their bank accounts, which were often huge.

The next year Sun took part in an anti-Manchu uprising in Canton. It failed, and Sun escaped to London. There, in an adventure that sounds right out of a British spy thriller, he was kidnapped and held prisoner in the Chinese Embassy. Fortunately, an English friend from medical school days intervened on his behalf. The Chinese released him, but the experience had given new drive to his anti-Manchu efforts—and a new talking point for his speeches. He recruited members for his society in Tokyo, and published a newspaper there. He traveled in Vietnam,

In her last years, the Empress Dowager Ci Xi grew quite fond of that western invention, the camera, and posed for it in many different costumes. More important, she began to realize after the Boxer Rebellion that China must learn from the West if the country was to be strong.

and in the United States. In the West he became the most famous Chinese of his day. "The George Washington of China" he was called.

Later, when he married the beautiful—and Christian —girl, Soong Qingling, daughter of one of the five most

Dr. Sun Yatsen, known as "the George Washington of China," led eleven unsuccessful revolutions against the Manchu Dynasty. The twelfth, in 1911, succeeded, the emperor abdicated, and a republic was proclaimed.

influential businessmen in China, his life seemed to Americans an ideal success story. Dreams piled on dreams in the secular and religious press. This charming crusader, with his Christian wife and capitalist father-in-law, would bring 400 million converts to the faith, and 400 million buyers to the marketplace. But reality turned out to be somewhat different from those dreams.

In Peking, neither George Washington nor Sun Yat-sen were exactly famous names. Sun was one of many "bandits" annoying the government, and America was one of many countries with possible lessons to teach. For the moment, there were other more pressing concerns.

In 1904, the Japanese decided to settle by force of arms a quarrel over the Chinese province of Manchuria. This province, the "old home" of the Manchus, is bordered by Korea on the southeast and by Siberia on the north. China had granted economic rights in Manchuria to Japan, and had allowed Russia to build a railroad across the province to the Pacific. Japan made demands of Russia, and when they were not met, enforced them by war *in Manchuria*. China was hardly consulted in the matter—a humiliating experience. And when Japan defeated Russia in the war, China realized again how far behind Japan she was in modernization.

The Empress Dowager Ci Xi died in 1908. The captive Emperor Guang Xu died in the same week. Those who had followed Ci Xi's career hardly raised an eyebrow at this coincidence, though the details of both deaths are unknown even now. Guang Xu's two-year-old nephew Pu Yi became emperor, with his father Prince Chun as regent.

The death of Ci Xi aroused hopes among all the reformers. Surely now they could proceed at a more rapid pace. Sun Yatsen continued his efforts to overthrow the dynasty. From time to time he would return to China and take part in a revolt. Eleven times, by his own count, he was unsuccessful. But more and more Chinese were growing dissatisfied with the weak leadership of the regent. The government convened "provincial assemblies" in 1909, and a "provisional national assembly" in 1910, to show it had not forgotten the promise of parliamentary rule by 1917. These assemblies had no authority to do anything except hold discussions, but their discussions, like those of the Continental Congress of the colonies before the American Revolution, helped to unify opinion. Revolts broke out in the south, in the west, and in the three important industrial cities of Wuchang, Hankou, and Hanyang in the Yangtze River basin. The government tried to put down all of these revolts, as usual, but in the three Yangtze cities the rebels soon got the upper hand. In Chinese history, October 10, 1911, the first day of the fighting there, is considered the beginning of the Revolution—the Chinese equivalent of the Battles of Lexington and Concord in Massachusetts. Double Ten Day (10/10/11), as it is called, is celebrated as the national holiday of the Republic of China.

On that day Sun Yatsen was in the United States, still raising money. He read of the success of his colleagues in a newspaper in Denver. He returned to China, and was elected provisional president of the revolutionary republican government the rebels set up.

The regent was fast losing control of the situation. He called on the strongest general in China to bring his army to the rescue. That general was Yuan Shikai, a brilliant leader who had been working since 1895 at mod-

General Yuan Shikai commanded the most modern military unit in China at the time of the 1911 Revolution. He made a bargain with Sun Yatsen: he would support the formation of a republic, in exchange for being named its first president.

ernizing the army corps for the province around Peking. His work had attracted the favorable attention of the court. He had also developed that army into a military unit intensely loyal to him personally. Yuan was intelligent, he was cunning, he was handsome and he was ambitious, to a degree rarely equaled in dynastic China. His ambition was nothing less than to become emperor. His troops were trained to protect the throne. He knew that if he sat on that throne, no soldiers in China could outfight them. But Yuan was wiser, or at least more patient, than the last would-be emperor Hong Xiuchuan, leader of the Taiping Rebellion. Yuan wanted to *rule* China. Therefore he had devoted himself to rising to power through the twisting channels of Peking politics, using his military strength only to command attention for what he said. Part of the military strategy he had learned decreed, "The wise general does not commit his forces to the battle too soon."

Yuan had had many invitations to commit his forces. In 1898, the Emperor Guang Xu had invited him to join in the Hundred Days of Reform, since Yuan was clearly in favor of modern methods for China. Instead of joining the reformers, Yuan had reported what was planned to his commander in chief, who in turn had reported it to Ci Xi. That bad day for reform was a good day for Yuan. During the Boxer Rebellion, Yuan had kept his force out of action, unwilling to fight against the Westerners and lose, unwilling to fight on the side of the Westerners and be branded a traitor by both sides. Many lesser generals had followed the same reasoning, and Yuan's inaction seems to have made the reunion no less sweet when Ci Xi returned to Peking in 1902.

In 1911 when the regent asked Yuan's help to put down Sun Yatsen's rebellion, Yuan replied that he was not really strong enough for the undertaking. He asked for command of all China's armed forces. The regent had no choice. The strengthened Yuan quickly recaptured the Yangtze cities held by the rebels. But he had no intention of presenting them to the regent or to the child emperor. By this time men were in arms all over China, declaring their independence of Manchu rule and killing Manchu garrisons. In December Yuan was given full power to negotiate a settlement with the rebels.

The settlement Yuan achieved was hardly what either side had hoped for. After some backing and filling, it amounted to this: 1) the Manchus would abdicate the throne; 2) Yuan would declare his support of the Republic; 3) Sun would resign as president in favor of Yuan. And so it was that the Manchus and the revolutionaries both recognized the military reality in China. Sun Yatsen helped draft a Republican Manifesto that echoes the American Declaration of Independence:

> . . . We now proclaim the resultant overthrow of
> the despotic sway wielded by the Manchu dynasty and
> the establishment of a Republic. . . . The policy
> of the Manchu dynasty has been one of unequivocal
> seclusion and unyielding tyranny. Beneath it we have
> bitterly suffered, and we now submit to the free people
> of the world the reasons justifying the revolution and
> the inauguration of our present government. . . .

The manifesto was proclaimed on January 5, 1912. Soon after that Sun went abroad again, to watch developments. On February 15, 1912, the provisional national assembly elected Yuan provisional president of China.

It soon became evident to anyone who really wanted

representative democratic government in China that General Yuan Shikai was not the man to provide it. He wanted to rule China. He possessed great power because of his army. It was very difficult for him to share that power with a cabinet, a premier, and a legislature, as was expected of him in the new government. And the thought that his power was subject to the will of the people, as expressed in elections, annoyed him. It annoyed him still more when the advocates of democracy, led by Sun Yatsen, reorganized as a political party, the Nationalist Party (Guomindang), and proceeded to win twice as many seats in the legislature as the party Yuan controlled.

Yuan met this rebuff in a thoroughly undemocratic way. He had the chief of the Nationalist Party assassinated, and ignored the legislature when it got in his way. The governors of the provinces were divided in allegiance. Some supported Yuan, some did not. Those who did not joined forces with the Nationalists and began a "Second Revolution," this time against Yuan. But Yuan defeated them in less than two months, and the legislature voted to change his title from provisional president to president.

It would be comforting to see these events as a struggle between a tyrant and a group of freedom fighters determined to establish democracy in China. Unfortunately the governors cannot bear such an honor. The provincial governments had no money to operate, once the abdication of the Manchus ended the traditional system of taxes for the emperor and his deputies. Yuan allowed the governors to raise money as they could, with the result that many of them quickly became rulers independent of the national government— "warlords." They maintained their power by the force of their troops, and they paid the troops by demanding tax money from the citizens. This was an old, old story in

China, whenever the central government was weak. Those warlords who opposed Yuan did so because they wanted more power themselves.

The legislators, both in Yuan's party and out of it, served democracy in an even worse way. There was no tradition of representative government in China to guide them. There was not even a body of revolutionary theory setting forth democratic goals. The Double Ten Day Revolution was fought to end the Manchu Dynasty. Its objectives beyond that were vague. Sun Yatsen had announced three "people's principles." The Nationalist Party adopted a national anthem for China based on his words. But the principles sang better than they worked for providing a new government for 400 million people. They were "Nationalism, Democracy, and the People's Livelihood," that last an expression of hope for social progress for the masses.

The legislators went to work with all the forms of Western lawmaking. But the bills that interested them most concerned their own salaries. When they considered proposals for education, army reform, railway construction and the innumerable other needs of the country, they openly offered their votes for sale. Their performance gave democracy a bad name in the minds of millions of Chinese, a bad name that it has never lived down.

Yuan saw his road clear at last. The Manchus were gone. Democracy was discredited. The country needed leadership. He would put an end to nonsense and become emperor—as he had long intended. As is usual with aspiring rulers, Yuan allowed underlings to beg him to "ascend the throne and save the country." He modestly declined several times, and finally was "persuaded." January 1, 1916 was set as the date for his assuming the ancient title.

The warlords were not pleased to think of Yuan with the prestige of that title. They managed to stir up enough trouble in the provinces to cause the ceremony to be postponed. And in June, Yuan sickened and died.

No man in China was strong enough to take his place. But for twelve years many men tried.

The death of Yuan Shikai, in June, 1916, was also the death of a central government for China. Yuan had governed China by the strength of his own army; the emperors before him had governed by virtue of traditional allegiance to the Confucian structure of society. But Yuan's vice-president, who succeeded him as president, had no army personally loyal to him, and his title commanded no respect at all among a people thoroughly disillusioned with what they had seen of democracy. Yuan had allowed the governors of the provinces to raise money for expenses any way they chose; the governors had used this freedom to build up their own military might, to the point where they were renamed "warlords."

A fairly typical career is that of Marshal Zhang Zuolin, warlord of China's rich industrial northeast region, Manchuria. Marshal Zhang began his climb to power as commander of the garrison of a little town near Shenyang, the capital city of Manchuria. Later he became military commander in Shenyang itself, where his strength grew through deals with the Japanese who were busy developing railroads

FIVE

Warlords, Student Power, and Nationalism

and expanding industry in the area. With the help of Japanese money, Zhang gained political control of all Manchuria, and governed it for his own ends. He professed allegiance to Peking, but it was clear his chief interest in the government there was his desire to control it.

A map of China for the decade 1916–1925 would show not one seat of power, but many. But the very weakness of the central government made possible a number of developments that a strong government might have squelched. For that decade was one of great change in the economics and politics of the world.

Those nations who saw enormous potential for profit in China were pleased by the government's weakness. While the Europeans were occupied with World War I, American financial interests negotiated several five-million-dollar loans for economic development, and sought concessions to build railroads. The Japanese also negotiated loans for rail, telegraph, forest and mining developments, with the condition attached that Japanese companies do the actual work —and collect much of the profit. Arrangements of this sort gave foreigners a large say in the economic life of China,

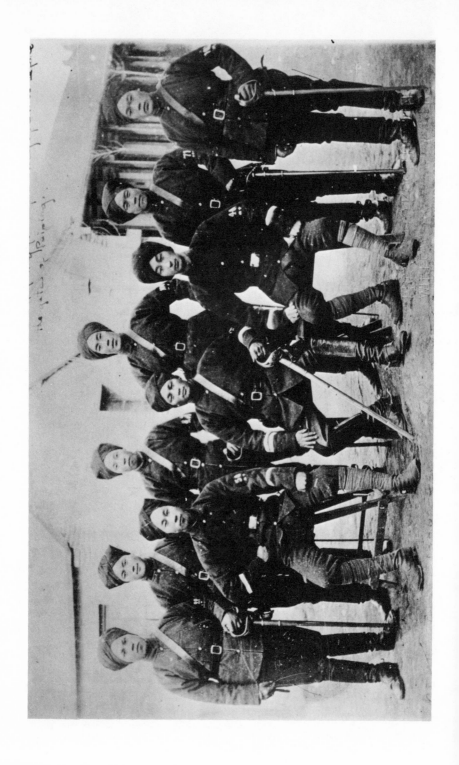

but on the other hand brought the country further into the industrial age.

For centuries the Chinese people had been divided into three main groups: peasants, landlords, and government officials. Now there were three additional groups, separated from the land that had always been the basis of Chinese society. There were industrial workers, desperately poor, and without fields to grow food to eat. There were financiers, enormously rich, but without the landlord's sense of responsibility for "his people." And there were students, educated in Western schools and searching for a way to put their new knowledge to work.

The students were keenly aware of the problems of their country. Their careers, and the future of China, depended on a new structure of society. Of course there was much disagreement among them over what the new form should be. But government by the gray-bearded sages was gone. Youth would play a major part from now on.

The most eloquent spokesman for youth was a thirty-five-year-old dean at the National University in Peking, Chen Duxiu. In 1915, Dean Chen founded a newspaper, *New Youth*. In it he wrote:

> *Youth is like early spring, like the rising sun, like trees and grass in bud, like a newly sharpened blade. It is the most valuable period of life. The function of youth in society is the same as that of a fresh and vital cell in a human body.*

Warlord Zhang Zuolin (seated, center) gained control of the province of Manchuria in 1916, after the death of President Yuan Shikai left China without a strong central government. Other military men ruled in other provinces until 1928.

*As for understanding what is right and wrong, in
order that you may make your choice, I carefully
propose the following six principles, and hope you
will give them your calm consideration. 1. Be
independent, not servile. 2. Be progressive, not
conservative. 3. Be aggressive, not retiring. 4. Be
cosmopolitan, not isolationist. 5. Be utilitarian, not
formalist. 6. Be scientific, not imaginative.*

Chinese youth gave Dean Chen's words an enthusiastic
welcome. The first issue of *New Youth* had to be reprinted
many times to fill the demand. Across the nation students
met again and again to discuss national policy.

By the year 1919, the subject that most held their
attention was the Versailles Peace Conference, where Great
Britain, France, Italy, the United States and Japan were
drawing up a treaty with Germany, vanquished in World
War I. Woodrow Wilson had proposed Fourteen Points
for international justice, and his vision of a League of Nations to maintain peace had captured the imagination of
the world. The Chinese students saw a possibility that Wilson's principle of "self-determination" for all nations would
apply to China, and foreign interference in China's life
would be ended. Indeed, in response to British and French
requests in 1917, China had sent a noncombatant labor
force of 200,000 volunteers to back up Allied armies fighting in France, and had actually declared war on Germany.
Her main objective in so doing was to earn a seat at the
peace conference so that her grievances would be heard.

The most urgent question in the minds of the Chinese
delegation to Versailles, and in the minds of the students
who avidly followed their negotiations, was the disposition
of the concessions granted to Germany in past years. In the

Chinese view, all the pieces of land granted to Germany for docks and railroads should revert to Chinese control. But these rights were a tempting prize. Shandong province, where the Germans had a coaling station at Qingdao for refueling their ships, juts out into the Yellow Sea, and thus commands the water route to Manchuria and to the port nearest Peking. Japan renewed a demand she had made almost as soon as the war began: "Turn over the German concessions to us."

The Versailles Peace Conference saw the end of many hopes. The victorious Allies indulged in "horse trading" for many bits of territory they wanted. And several prominent figures in the weak Peking government looked on Japan as a powerful support for their personal ambitions. The Chinese delegates received no strong backing from their government, and in the end Japan got what she had asked for.

The students were sickened by this news. On May 3, 1919, a group of a thousand, mostly from the National University in Peking, met to discuss the matter. One of them described the meeting:

We first discussed the problem of our national crisis and we all agreed that the Shandong problem was caused by corruption and injustice, and that we as students must fight to show the world that "might should never be right!" . . . [We resolved to meet] on May 4, the students of all the schools in Peking, at The Square of Heavenly Peace to show our discontent by a great mass parade.

During the meeting, a student of the Law School deliberately cut open his finger and wrote on the wall

in blood "Return our Qingdao." The students were
all quiet.

The next morning, Sunday, May 4, representatives
from thirteen colleges and universities in the Peking area
met to organize the demonstration in an orderly way. That
afternoon, more than 3,000 students assembled in the appointed square, the largest in Peking, and the traditional
place for mass meetings. A *Manifesto of All the Students
of Peking* was distributed:

> *Japan's demand for the possession of Qingdao and
> other rights in Shandong is now going to be acceded
> to in the Paris Peace Conference. Her diplomacy has
> scored a great victory; and ours has led to a great
> failure. . . . Accordingly, we students today are
> making a demonstration march to the Allied legations,
> asking the Allies to support justice. . . . Today we
> swear two solemn oaths with all our countrymen:
> (1) China's territory may be conquered, but it cannot
> be given away; (2) The Chinese people may be
> massacred, but they will not surrender. Our country
> is about to be annihilated. Up, brethren!*

The police of Peking advised the student leaders not
to hold the demonstration, but took no active steps to stop
it. For the first part of the afternoon, the students maintained order themselves. They marched to the gate into
the Legation Quarter, a section that was still protected
by grants of extraterritoriality. The Legation police force
stopped the body of students, but allowed a small group
of representatives to seek meetings with the ministers of
the United States, Britain, France and Italy. All these
diplomats were absent from the quarter, it seemed, on

this Sunday afternoon. The students' primary objective of marching through the Legation Quarter to show their indignation at the Versailles decision was thwarted. Some students then suggested that they might protest at the Chinese Foreign Ministry, or directly to the pro-Japanese officials, whom the students considered traitors. Accordingly, the demonstration moved toward the Foreign Ministry. At the house of the Minister of Communications, one of the "traitors" they sought, a group of students gained entrance, but the minister escaped. The students, their frustration rising, set fire to the house. Another group found another pro-Japanese official and beat him. One student was injured as the Peking police finally began to restrain the crowd; he died three days later. Thirty-two students were arrested. By nightfall the demonstration was over. But it had an effect far beyond anything its organizers could have dreamed of.

News of the May Fourth demonstration spread throughout China. Here was an indication that students could work together for goals they believed in. Older intellectuals who shared their Western ideas made common cause with them. All over the country the students and intellectuals met together to consider how to strengthen China. They enlisted the support of the merchants and financiers, and for the first time began to look for support among the masses of China—masses illiterate and long considered without opinions, but numerous beyond the populace of any other nation. Protest strikes and demonstrations were held in other cities and in June a general strike in Shanghai secured the release of the thirty-two students arrested. The May Fourth Movement, as these activities came to be called, came close to uniting China in genuine nationalistic fervor.

All those who adopted the principles of the May

Fourth Movement agreed that China must be strong. The problem came in knowing the right path to that objective. Democracy as practiced in the United States appealed to the Chinese no longer. The 1911 Republic proclaimed by Sun Yatsen had been patterned after the American one and had failed miserably. Woodrow Wilson had been unable to rally enough support for his principle of "self-determination" to protect China's interests at Versailles.

Another great revolution had just taken place, however, in Russia, seeking to replace a hereditary tyranny by a rule of the people. Perhaps the model for China was to be found there. The Russian revolutionists had set up a government—the Soviet Union—based on the political theories of Karl Marx and Nikolai Lenin, including the theory that all property should be held in common by the people—Communism. The followers of Marx and Lenin in many countries had formed a political organization, the Communist International, to spread their teachings throughout the world. Their success in Russia was their most spectacular achievement to date, but their "missionaries" were active in many countries. Chinese who had studied in Europe had heard their theories, along with those of other political and economic analysts.

Less than two months after the May Fourth demonstration, in the Soviet Union the new Communist government decreed an end to "all the secret treaties concluded with Japan, China and the former Allies; treaties by which the Czar's government, together with its allies, through force and corruption, enslaved the peoples of the Orient, and especially the Chinese nation, in order to profit the Russian capitalists, the Russian landlords, and the Russian generals." This declaration was a master stroke. "Landlords" and "generals" were exactly the group the Chinese

intellectuals held responsible for the sorrows of their coun-
try. The next year the Society for the Study of Marxist
Theory was established at the National University in
Peking, by Li Dazhao, the university librarian, and others.
One of Li's followers was a brilliant twenty-six-year-old stu-
dent from Hunan province in the south named Mao
Zedong.

Similar study societies were formed in other parts of
China. The Communist International was eager to supply
teachers and books for their studies. By July 1921, it
seemed there were enough Marxists in China to form their
own Chinese Communist Party. Librarian Li, and Dean
Chen, whose words in *New Youth* had so stirred the students, were not present in Shanghai for the actual formation of the party, but they gave their blessing.

Young Mao was named a party organizer for his native
province of Hunan. He was probably the most effective
organizer Communism has ever had. The party went on
with its work of enlisting more members. In three years
there were about 600 Chinese Communists. In thirty years,
the party was to control the entire country, with a population estimated then at 600 million.

The members of the fledgling Chinese Communist
Party advocated revolution. The weak government at Peking
seemed little more than a puppet of Japan. Advisers from
the Communist International pointed out that there was
another group in China that had been advocating revolution
for decades: the followers of Sun Yatsen. Although they
had met setback after setback, their numbers were considerable, and Sun himself had prestige both in China and
abroad. What Sun seemed to lack was organizing ability
and a definite program. The Communist International ex-
celled in those areas. Good strategy for the Chinese Com-

munists, said their advisers, was to join forces with Sun's Nationalist Party.

Since the death of General Yuan Shikai in 1916, Sun had been negotiating with the warlords in the southern provinces around Canton. Several times he had proclaimed a new Republic, backed by one general or another; none had lasted long. In 1922, the government of the Soviet Union sent one of its ablest diplomats, Adolph Joffe, to confer with Sun and offer him help in "organization." The Soviet Union, Joffe explained, wanted to see established a "strong, united and democratic China, free from the menace of militarism and imperialism." In fact, he continued, the Russians, having overthrown the imperial Czars, wanted to see an end to imperial designs throughout Asia.

No one quite believed Joffe's unselfish declarations. In fact, on the same trip he also stopped in Peking to confer with the "militarists" in the government there. Any realist who looked at the map of Asia could see that the young government in Moscow would be just as interested as the czarist government before it in maintaining access to the Pacific Ocean. The ice-free Russian port of Vladivostok depended for its usefulness on a rail line from Moscow, and the most direct route crossed Manchuria. A strong China, friendly to the Soviet Union, might put an end to Japanese meddling in that region.

Sun Yatsen saw that. There was much in Marxist theory that repelled him. But he was interested in the help Joffe offered. His experience with the warlords around Canton had shown that a new government for China must have military strength behind it if it was to endure. Every alliance he had made with a warlord had failed. Could he now give his political party its own military arm? In January, 1923, Sun and Joffe issued a joint declaration, stating that the "chief and immediate aim of China is the achievement of national union and national independence," and that the Nationalist movement "could depend on the aid of Russia." Sun sent a small delegation to Moscow to study the organization of the Soviet army. And advisers came to Canton to help shape the Nationalists into a disciplined party. Good strategy for the Nationalists, said these advisers, was to join forces with the skilled political organizers of the Chinese Communist Party.

And so it was that in the first Congress of the Nationalist Party, held in Canton in January 1924, Sun's followers and the Communists agreed to work together "for the National Revolution." They organized protest groups of peasants and industrial workers so effectively that the foreign merchants in Canton and Shanghai began to realize that "anti-imperialism" was more than a slogan.

When Sun's military-study delegation returned from Moscow, the Nationalists set up the Whampoa Military Academy for the training of officers. The Russians assisted. And the commandant of the academy was a thirty-eight-year-old member of the delegation, Sun's aide, Chiang Kaishek.

hiang Kaishek was not particularly well known when he became the first commandant of the new Whampoa Military Academy in 1924. But in the next twenty-five years he was to become the man who most nearly symbolized China in the eyes of the world. Sun Yatsen and Yuan Shikai were names recognized by those who followed news of foreign affairs; Generalissimo Chiang Kaishek, and his nickname "G-mo," became household words. Grade school pupils in America heard his virtues praised. Foot soldiers of many nations, suddenly transported to fight World War II in the least attractive parts of Asia, blamed him for all their troubles. Even today there is little agreement among historians about his contribution to China.

Chiang was born in 1887 in a village south of Shanghai. He was too young to understand the news of the Hundred Days of Reform in 1898 and at thirteen he could only dream of feats of battle during the Boxer Rebellion. But by the time he was eighteen, he had heard enough of Sun Yatsen's doctrines to believe that his country needed a new and better government. He resolved to be a soldier in the revolution he was sure would come.

The Nationalist Party Gains Control

Halfway measures never appealed to Chiang. Once he decided he would be a fighting man, he set about making himself the most effective fighter possible. The best soldiers in Asia were the Japanese; China's few expert generals had taken their military training at the Japanese Military Cadets Academy in Tokyo. Chiang resolved to study there.

First he learned to speak Japanese. He passed the academy's entrance examinations. Then for four years he applied himself to his military lessons there, and put up with the rigid discipline of the Japanese military system. It was not an easy four years. But when the revolution he expected broke out, on Double Ten Day, October 10, 1911, he was ready.

As soon as the news of fighting reached Tokyo, Chiang returned to China. His first assignment in the revolution was to capture Hangzhou, the capital of his native Zhejiang province. He commanded only a hundred men, but the imperial army defending the town included many men sympathetic to the rebels' cause. The fighting lasted only one day, and Chiang was a hero. He was given a regiment to command.

Sun Yatsen's revolution succeeded in ending the Man-

*Chiang Kaishek had barely graduated from military
academy when the 1911 Revolution began, but his
capture of the city of Hangzhou made him a hero
overnight, and started him on the path to eventual
rule of China.*

chu Dynasty, but it did not succeed in replacing it by
democracy. At one point Chiang put aside his military dreams and went to work in the financial world
of Shanghai, where he made influential friends among that
new group in China, the Chinese capitalists. But Sun kept
calling him back to fighting: he was one of the best trained

soldiers he had. After one particular defeat, Sun spent two months on a ship in Canton harbor, watching the turn of events. He again called for Chiang, who came and spent that time with him as his aide. It was probably in those two months that Sun developed his great confidence in the younger man. That was in 1922 and it was two years later that Chiang was named commandant of the new military academy at Whampoa. Classes began on June 16, 1924 and the first class graduated four months later. Students divided their time between military classes in tactics and discipline, and political indoctrination.

In October, 1924, the cadets had a chance to practice what they had learned. The foreign merchants sought to expel Sun from Canton, as he had been expelled often before. The men of Whampoa, fighting side by side with groups of workers and peasants organized by the Communists, disarmed the merchants' militia. The following February they repelled a more serious threat from a provincial warlord who sought to control the city. Peasants all over the province helped the Nationalist troops, setting a pattern that was to give the Nationalist Party eventual control of the entire country.

Sun Yatsen could see his ideas taking concrete form at last. As agreed at the First Congress of the Nationalist Party in 1924, Nationalists and Communists were working together to oppose foreign meddling, to demand better conditions for workers, to change the old relations of landlord and peasant. The People's Livelihood, the third and vaguest of Sun's People's Principles, now seemed more than a distant dream. But Sun himself was gravely ill. At this point he accepted an invitation to go to Peking to confer with the coalition of warlords who controlled the central government—a government that was by now only an empty form. Before the conference could yield any results, Sun died on March 12, 1925. The timing of his death could not have been better for his future reputation. Political divisions in the Nationalist ranks were just around the corner, but Sun was spared the agony of choosing sides, and each faction has claimed him as prophet and hero.

Several leaders of the Nationalist Party considered themselves the logical successor to Sun. Chiang Kaishek was one of them, but for a time the party limited his activities to the military area. In 1925, recruiting new members was the major concern. The Communists organized workers in the factories of Shanghai. In May, the workers in the Japanese-owned cotton mills there went on strike. In the International Settlement, where the foreigners lived protected by extraterritoriality, a striker was killed. Student protests followed. When the demonstrators reached the police station in the Settlement, they were fired on by the police, who were under British command; thirteen demonstrators were killed. Three weeks later fifty-two Chinese were killed in a similar protest in Canton. These killings gave a great impetus to the nationalistic, antiforeign feeling, and a great impetus to the growth of the Nationalist party. On July 1, 1925, the party proclaimed at Canton, as it had done several times before, the Nationalist Government of China. This time the Nationalists intended to make it the government of all China, by force.

The Second Congress of the Nationalist Party, held in Canton in January 1926, was marked by considerable disagreement about both methods and objectives. Three factions were represented. The Chinese Communist members were continuing to organize the industrial workers for class warfare. At the opposite extreme, a "right wing" of the Nationalists proposed a policy of "national unity" that would bring Chinese of all classes together to work against foreign influence—against the European merchants with their warships at their backs, and also against the Communists with their advisers from Moscow. The third faction, the so-called "left wing" of the Nationalists, was a group trying to keep the whole party together in order to give maximum support to the Nationalist army.

Chiang Kaishek no doubt agreed with the right wing; his family were merchants, and he himself still had many friends in the financial community in Shanghai. But he wanted Soviet arms and money for his troops, and he had seen in his first military command in 1911 how easy it is to take a city when its defenders are actually in sympathy with the attackers. Communist organizers were building up sympathy for the Nationalists in all the major cities. Therefore Chiang publicly supported the idea of keeping the Communists as active members of the Nationalist Party. And he urged the party to launch at once its "Northern Expedition" to expand its military control from Canton over the rest of the country.

The question of Sun's successor was still not settled. But, one by one, Chiang's rivals were implicated in assassinations and plots, and discredited. On June 5, 1926, Chiang got the job he really wanted: Commander in Chief of the National Revolutionary Army for the Northern Expedition. If he controlled the army, he cared little for the niceties of political discussion. On July 9, the expedition was launched.

City after city fell to the Nationalist army, as troops and citizens enlisted under Chiang's banner, and local warlords either offered him allegiance or fled. By March, 1927, he had reached the richest prize of all, Shanghai, the country's financial center and most modern port.

The events of the next month have been examined over and over again by scholars, in an attempt to find out what really happened, and to interpret Chiang's actions. There is little agreement on interpretation. But the broad outline of events now seems clear. As an industrial city, Shanghai was a fertile field for labor unions. Long before there was a Chinese Communist Party, reformers had organized the workers in Shanghai to fight for improvements in the miserable conditions in the factories. The Communists brought increased skill to the work of the organization.

The growing strength of the workers had rallied other groups in Shanghai to oppose them: the factory owners, the Chinese financiers, the local warlord and the local leaders of the criminal underworld, all of whom saw their own power threatened. In the International Settlement, 40,000 foreign troops assembled to protect the Europeans —to save them from the workers, from the Communists, and from the Nationalists, all of whom were preaching anti-imperialism and workers' rights.

On March 21, 1927, the workers staged a city-wide strike that brought all industry to a halt; then they seized control of all the government offices and police stations in the Chinese part of the city. Chiang's forces entered the paralyzed city without opposition, to the cheers of the strikers. But in the next week, he spent more time in conference with the financiers than with the Communists and the labor leaders. Some Communists began to express doubts about Chiang, but the Communist International, under its new leader Joseph Stalin, insisted that cooperation with him would lead to success. On April 5, Stalin said in reply to questions about China:

*Why drive away the Right when we have the majority
and the Right listens to us? The peasant needs a
worn-out jade [horse] as long as she is necessary. He
does not drive her away. . . . At present, we need
the Right. It has capable people, who still direct the
army and lead it against the imperialists. . . .
Also, they have connections with the rich merchants
and can raise money from them. So they have to be
utilized to the end, squeezed out like a lemon, and
then flung away.*

When the workers in Shanghai became even more ap-
prehensive about Chiang's intentions, the Executive Committee of the Communist International sent this directive:
"Open struggle is not to be launched at this time (in view
of the very unfavorable change in the relationship of
forces). Arms must not be given up but in any extremity,
they must be hidden." And so the Communists dutifully
hid or buried what few modern weapons they had. By
April 12, most of their weapons were safely stored out of
reach. At 4:00 A.M. on that day, a bugle sounded at Chiang
Kaishek's headquarters in Shanghai, and all over the city
the headquarters of workers' organizations found themselves under attack. Who were the attackers? "Anti-communists," say some. "Underworld gangs," say others, or
"Chiang's own soldiers." The truth was washed away in
the blood of three hundred summary executions. On that
one day, the strongest citadel of the Chinese Communist
Party was destroyed.

The reign of terror dissolved the cohesive power of the
only force in China that could have opposed Chiang's plans,
the organized workers. Their leaders were now dead or in
hiding, and the workers felt betrayed by the Communist

Soong Meiling married Chiang Kaishek on December 1, 1927. The Soong family had great financial power in China; Madame Chiang's connections, persuasiveness and determination were of enormous help to her husband in his rise to power.

International as well as by Chiang. Their fighting spirit was gone.

Chiang lost no time in announcing his alliance with the most powerful financiers in Shanghai, including the

Soong family. On April 18, he set up his own government in the city of Nanking, China's ancient capital. From that moment, the Nationalist Party was Chiang Kaishek. The Chinese Communists would all be expelled from party membership, and the "Left Wing" could come over to the right or go hang.

On December 1, 1927, Chiang married the youngest daughter of the Soong family, Meiling. The Soongs were Christians, and Meiling's mother had consented to the marriage only on condition that Chiang give serious thought to becoming a Christian. Chiang kept his promise, and three years later was baptized.

In 1928, Chiang continued his march north and took Peking. Since he had made Nanking his capital, he changed the name Peking, meaning "northern capital," to Peiping, meaning "northern peace." It seemed for a time that peace might be a reality in China, for the first time in many years.

Although several warlords declared their support of the "Left Wing," Chiang controlled the Yangtze River Valley and Shanghai, and therefore controlled the economy of China. The warlords would come over to his side soon enough. And if they didn't, he had behind him all the troops who had rallied to his banner as he marched from Canton to Shanghai. He had said in 1923 that warfare was the only way the Nationalist Party could gain control of China; he had carried on the war, and won. In the long run his raw strength was the decisive factor in politics.

The Russian advisers left for "conferences" at home. The Chinese Communists who escaped execution had no such easy withdrawal open to them.

ao Zedong, China's future ruler, had watched Chiang Kaishek's rise to power from a distance. In 1927, when Chiang gained control of Shanghai and destroyed the Communist Party's strength among factory workers, Mao was recruiting party members among the farmers of southwest China. He was enormously successful at recruiting work. And his success changed the whole shape of Communist thought.

Mao was born on December 26, 1893 in the village of Shaoshan in Hunan province in south central China. His father was a dealer in pigs and rice. By hard work and thrift the family saved enough money to realize the ancient Chinese ambition of buying a piece of land. When Zedong, the eldest child, was five years old he started to work in the rice fields. Later, two brothers and a sister joined him. The family raised more rice than they needed and sold the surplus for cash, which they lent to others, as was the custom in China, at exorbitant rates of interest. Their savings grew.

At the age of seven, Zedong began his schooling with a tutor in the village. Before long he was keeping the

SEVEN

Communist Defiance

financial accounts for his father. The Mao family continued to prosper, and rented out some of their land to tenants. It was customary in Hunan for the owner to charge as rent as much as sixty percent of the crop the land produced, leaving only forty percent for the tenants. As Mao grew older he was responsible for collecting this rent. So he saw at first hand the situation of the peasants. And he did not like what he saw.

The story is told that one day when the rice was being threshed it began to rain. Every available hand was needed to get the rice indoors. Instead of helping his own family, young Mao helped the tenants. Later he explained to his father that the tenants' need for the rice was greater.

Mao had an enormous appetite for reading, and it was obvious his good mind deserved more education than he could get in his village. So in 1910, when he was sixteen, his family sent him to school in his mother's hometown. There he was particularly interested by a collection of biographies of such heroes of the West as George Washington, Napoleon, and Peter the Great. He also studied the writing of the scholars who were trying to reform Chinese society, including the leader of the Hundred Days of Reform of 1898, Kang Yuwei.

In October, 1911, when the followers of Sun Yatsen began their revolution against the Manchu Dynasty, Mao enlisted in their army. He was a soldier of the revolution until he was demobilized in February, 1912. He returned to his studies, and in 1913 was admitted to the Teachers' Training School in the provincial capital of Changsha. He continued to win recognition, and in June 1917, a year before he graduated from the school's five-year course, he was elected one of thirty-four model students (out of 400). He developed a clear style of writing, and that same spring had an article published in the magazine *New Youth*, edited by Dean Chen of the National University in Peking. His subject was the importance of developing a strong body. For Mao, despite his avid reading, was no bookworm. He loved physical activity, particularly swimming, a sport he practiced to an advanced age. He took a cold bath every day of the year, for toughening. In the summer vacation of 1916, he and a friend went on a long hike through their native province of Hunan, climbing mountains, living on beans and water or meals Mao could earn by writing scrolls for farmers along the way.

Mao's reading made him well aware of all the ferment in China since the Manchu Dynasty had abdicated in 1911. He knew that the efforts of Sun Yatsen and other reformers to give China some form of representative government had not had much success, and that the armies of the provincial warlords were the real power in China just then.

In April 1918, just before graduation, Mao and twelve friends formed the New Citizens Society in Changsha to train members to be good citizens of a new China. The Society held discussion meetings every week or so and grew slowly.

Mao Zedong was in college at the time students first became a major political force in China. In 1919 he joined the Society for the Study of Marxist Theory at Peking University and went on to become the most effective spokesman the Communists had.

Mao's education had prepared him for a career as a teacher, and the subject matter that interested him most was politics. He graduated just at the moment when students were becoming a major force in the political life of

China. In September, 1918, he went to Peking for the first of several visits to the National University. His article in *New Youth* gave him an entree to Dean Chen. He also met the university librarian Li Dazhao, who found a job for him checking out books that paid just enough for him to live on.

The next year when Chen and Li formed the Society for the Study of Marxist Theory, Mao joined it. His political career developed rapidly. In 1920, he organized similar societies in Hunan province, and in 1921, he worked to strengthen the newly formed Chinese Communist Party. In 1922, he directed a strike of coal miners, and by April, 1923, his activities had attracted enough attention for the governor of Hunan to order his arrest.

Mao escaped from Hunan, and in the summer of 1923, was elected to the Central Committee of the Chinese Communist Party, and given responsibility for coordinating work with the Nationalist Party. That was one job Mao was not suited for, however, and after a year he returned to what interested him most: teaching politics to the peasants of China. Some leaders in both parties sneered at that work, and regarded Mao as something of a country hick himself.

But Mao had quickly perceived that Communism could not succeed in China in the form taught by Marx and Lenin. Their doctrines and their methods were directed toward changing the industrial society of Europe, by organizing industrial workers. But China in the 1920s was not an industrial society, despite many efforts to introduce Western ways. Less than one percent of her population worked in factories. The peasant farming the land was still the basis of China's strength, as had been true for thousands of years.

In February, 1927, Mao wrote a long and brilliant essay, "The Peasant Movement in Hunan." He explained the basic impossibility of applying Communism in its "classic" form to China's needs, and advocated greater emphasis on improving the lot of the farmers. In Mao's province only a fifth of the people owned the land they farmed. The rest worked as tenants. In addition, the tenants rather than the owners paid the heavy taxes on the land. In years of good crops, constant work by every member of a family produced a basic living. In bad years, tens of thousands of people starved, while the landlords and the gentry —the local officials—lived off their accumulated wealth. Here, said Mao, was the situation that communism should seek to correct. Specifically, the party should work for an equitable distribution of the land among the people.

Brilliant though Mao's essay was, it directly contradicted the basic Communist tenets taught in Moscow. It gained Mao a reputation as a heretic in the party. And the party, still taking orders from Moscow, continued to work for control of the industrial cities. Most of that work was wiped out by Chiang Kaishek's executioners in 1927. But Moscow continued sending orders.

In September, 1927, Mao dutifully organized in Hunan province an armed force for an Autumn Harvest Uprising, which destroyed a section of a railroad supplying coal for industry. But the uprising was soon suppressed, and Mao led as much of his force as survived to safety in the mountains on the border between Hunan and Jiangxi province. The party promptly expelled him from its council.

In December of the same year, the Chinese Communists' best general, Zhu De, led an uprising in Canton, which was equally unsuccessful. It was the second time in five months that orders from Moscow had sent Zhu De on an impossible mission. In January, he joined Mao in his mountain stronghold. Now the party's most effective political organizer and its most skillful military strategist were united. The future of Chinese Communism lay in their hands—though it was several years before the upper levels of the party admitted that reality.

The two men combined their forces to form a military unit they called the Fourth Red Army. Following party practice, the army had a dual command: a military leader in General Zhu, and a political leader in Mao. Soldiers numbered about 10,000 at first. That number grew steadily with the arrival of additional refugees from Chiang Kai-shek's anti-Communist campaign. One of the ablest additions was Zhou Enlai, a handsome, urbane member of the party Central Committee, who had organized the factory workers in Shanghai before Chiang took the city. Zhou had spent several years in Europe in his twenties. His breadth of knowledge coupled with his natural charm were large assets in any dealings with non-communists, and he soon became the party's number one "negotiator."

Six months later, in July, 1928, Mao and Zhu established a government in Jiangxi province patterned after the provincial governments the Communists had established in Russia. The basic building block of the government was a "soviet," or council for each town, composed of representatives of the peasants, the workers and the army. This soviet decided all matters for the town, and sent delegates to provincial congresses. And so on up the ladder, to national congresses and an international congress of delegates where world Communist policy was set.

That same summer, other Communists set up a second soviet government in Shaanxi province in China's northwest. These two governments became the rallying points for Chinese Communism—and the focus for Chiang's efforts to destroy the party.

The Fourth Red Army was very small in comparison to the force Chiang commanded, and it had no regular source of weapons. But Zhu and Mao developed a very effective technique of guerrilla warfare. In the mountains they had chosen for their headquarters, conventional warfare was impossible. There was no room for a full-scale battle, where overwhelming numbers would surely win. The fighting took place in narrow valleys and passes, a few men fighting with a few. The communists studied the terrain well, and were expert at setting up ambush after ambush, where the enemy was killed and their weapons captured.

As Mao himself explained the strategy:

When the enemy advances, we retreat. When he camps, we harass. When he tires we attack. And when he retreats, we pursue. Our weapons are supplied us by the enemy.

These words became the basis for a rousing marching song, eventually the Chinese Communist anthem. Where the Nationalist anthem, based on Sun Yatsen's Three Peoples' Principles, was as stately and stuffy as "My Country 'Tis of Thee," the Communist song was as lively and confident as the United States Marine Hymn. Comparison of the two songs tells a lot about the difference of the two parties' appeal to China's millions.

Guerrilla warfare produced no major victories of the sort the Communist International longed for. But it served to keep Communism alive in China. All the Chinese Communists, no matter how critical they were of Mao's unorthodox methods, realized his army was their only hope.

In 1931, a new enemy distracted Chiang's attention from the Communists for a time. Japan invaded Manchuria, China's rich industrial northeast corner. The invasion was the first step in a Japanese plan to gain control of all of East Asia. Faced with two enemies, Chiang made a basic decision: he would concentrate his military force first on destroying his domestic foes, the Communists, so that he would have a unified China behind him for a war with Japan. So he ordered his armies to withdraw from Manchuria, where Japan soon established a puppet government. Chiang appealed to the League of Nations for help, but the League was not strong enough to take effective action.

Although his decision was immensely unpopular with patriotic Chinese, Chiang returned to what he called his "bandit suppression campaigns." (He never dignified the Communists by treating them as political adversaries—only as outlaws.) Four campaigns failed. For campaign number five, in 1934, he sent 150,000 troops, with directions to carry out a slow, steady encirclement of the entire Jiangxi soviet area. The plan would take time, but it was bound to succeed. The Nationalist troops even built concrete blockhouses along the siege line, strong enough to withstand guerrilla attacks.

Meanwhile a power struggle had been going on inside the Communist base. By 1932, the theorists in Moscow recognized that Communist power in China's industrial

In 1931, Japan invaded China's northeast province of Manchuria, and gradually pushed south. Chiang Kaishek offered little resistance, because he believed his first responsibility was to annihilate his foes at home, the Chinese Communists.

cities was not growing but dissolving. Consequently, they once more sent a military adviser to China, and directed the leading Chinese party members to accompany him to Mao's headquarters. Moscow wanted the Red Army to abandon its guerrilla warfare and take fixed battle positions, in the hope of expanding the area under Communist control. There followed a year of political maneuvering. The party leaders managed to wrest control of the army from Mao, whom they still regarded as a heretic. And they did win a few battles.

Then came Chiang's encirclement plan in 1934, and everyone saw it was futile to attempt even to hold the Jiangxi base. Mao advised that the Red Army should slip through the siege line in small units, to reassemble elsewhere. This would minimize losses and preserve the army's strength almost intact. The party leadership agreed that the Army should escape Chiang's encirclement, but insisted that it break out as a unit.

On October 15, 1934, the escape began. The army numbered 85,000 soldiers. With them went 15,000 civilians, officials of the party and of the Jiangxi soviet, and 35 women, wives of high officials.

Losses in the breakout were heavy, as Mao had predicted. Furthermore, once the army had escaped the encirclement, the party leaders had no clear idea of what to do next. By January, 1935, those leaders were thoroughly discredited. They had lost the party's principal base, and much of the army's strength. Mao insisted that a party conference be held to set new objectives. At that conference, held in the town of Zunyi, Mao was elected Chairman of the Political Bureau (the Politburo), the highest political office in the party. This election recognized for the first time that he was the number one Communist in China. The conference elected as his deputy Zhou Enlai.

Mao immediately gave the Communists the sense of purpose they so badly needed at the low point in their fortunes. The only remaining base of Communist power in China was the other soviet established in 1928, in Shaanxi province in northwest China. Beyond Shaanxi, in the northeast, the Japanese invaders were gradually extending their control from Manchuria over more and more territory with little opposition from Chiang Kaishek. Mao proposed a new slogan for his men: "Head north to fight the Japanese." It had a powerful appeal, for it suggested renewed strength for the army from a union with comrades in Shaanxi, and a patriotic objective that would keep men going through many hardships.

Mao was well aware of what the hardships would be. Reaching Shaanxi required a roundabout journey of 6,000 miles—twice the distance from New York to San Francisco. The country they would have to cross is some of the wildest in the world. Here torrential rivers pour down out of the Himalaya, the highest mountains on this planet. In some places, vast swamps block travel. In others, deserts stretch for hundreds of miles. The inhabitants are fierce tribes, ruled at that time by independent tribal chiefs or by provincial warlords who viewed any strangers as a threat to their authority.

Led by Mao, the Communists began this journey, a journey that gave China a new epic of heroism, and the Communist party a unified strength it had never had before. This great story goes by a simple name, the Long March.

According to party records, Mao and his followers crossed eighteen mountain chains and twenty-four rivers, fought the armies of ten warlords, and occupied en route sixty-two cities. Chiang Kaishek never stopped trying to destroy them. He recalled later that he himself had a pilot fly him over the line of march so he could see his enemy in retreat. They flew for two hours over the marching columns.

The Long March captured the imagination of the world, as the story became known. One incident in particular has been used time after time as an example of bravery and determination.

In May 1935 the march came to the Dadu River, a swift stream dashing between steep canyon walls. Chiang's men knew the Communists must cross this river, so they installed machine guns at the far end of the only bridge across it, at the little town of Luding. The bridge was a chain bridge, consisting of thirteen heavy chains strung from one side of the gorge to the other, supporting a wooden walkway. Chiang's soldiers tore up sections of the walkway to slow down any men advancing across the bridge, and make them easy targets for the machine guns.

Mao's army quickly sized up the situation. Bad as it was, any delay would only allow the enemy to call for reinforcements. Under cover of darkness, an attack squad of twenty volunteers started across the gorge, not over the bridge but hanging from the chains and inching forward hand over hand. Chiang's men opened fire, and lighted torches to see their targets better. Eventually, most of the volunteers reached the bank and one managed to land a grenade in the machine gun position. Mao's men poured over the bridge and the Dadu was crossed.

On countless walls in China, posters show that attack squad swinging along the chains, their faces illuminated by the red glow of the torches. As the distinguished French writer Andre Malraux observes, "It is the most famous legend of Red China. In the memory of every Chinese, that string of dangling men swaying toward freedom seem to be brandishing aloft the chains to which they cling."

On the marchers went, fighting sometimes against Chiang, sometimes against the local inhabitants, and always against hostile nature. Thousands died in battle. Thousands more died from the hardships of the journey.

The only food the army had was what they could get from the people who lived along their route. That has been true of armies in all countries and ages. But Mao took an approach to the problem that was new in China. Most armies simply took what they needed by force from the peasants, with the result that the Chinese viewed the approach of any army as a disaster comparable to a swarm of locusts. Soldiers in China were traditionally regarded as the lowest class in the social structure. Mao was leading an army, but he never lost sight of his greater goal of leading a party that would rule China. Since he viewed the peasants as the great source of strength for Chinese Communism, whenever possible on the Long March he tried to maintain good relations with them. He forbade his men to take anything. Instead they should explain that they were fighting to deliver all Chinese from oppression, and attempt to win support. If that failed, they were to pay for the food they needed.

This approach had a double effect. People all along the route of the Long March remembered the Communist army as different from any other they had ever known. And Mao and the leaders under him gained deep insight into the mentality of the peasants.

In October, 1935, Mao and his men reached the Communist base in Shaanxi Province. The Long March had lasted a whole year. Of the 100,000 men who broke through the Nationalist encirclement in Jiangxi, 23,000 completed the journey. Among the leaders were Zhou Enlai, Zhu De, Deng Xiaopeng, Liu Shaoqi and Lin Biao.

These men had faced great danger and hardship together and had survived. The experience of the march bound them together with bonds that were to endure for decades.

In Shaanxi, the Communists gained a short breathing spell to recover from their ordeal. They captured the town of Yan'an, and made it their new base. Chiang Kaishek never relented in his determination to annihilate them, but the general he had assigned to Shaanxi did not share Chiang's conviction that defeat of the Communists was the Nationalist army's primary goal. That general was a Manchurian, still smarting from Chiang's abandonment of Manchuria to the Japanese without a fight. His name was Zhang Xueliang, known as "the Young Marshal" to distinguish him from his father, Marshal Zhang Zuolin, the former warlord of Manchuria.

Almost immediately after Mao and his men arrived in Shaanxi, they made contact with the Young Marshal at his headquarters in the provincial capital of Xi'an. They urged him to join them, adopt their slogan, and "head north to fight the Japanese." For most of 1936, Marshal Zhang debated and did nothing. During this time, Communist strength was growing as Red Army units from various provinces joined Mao and Zhu.

In October, 1936, Chiang Kaishek visited Zhang to plan another "bandit suppression campaign" against the Communists—campaign number six. The Marshal and Chiang discussed the desirability of fighting the Japanese, but Chiang held to his idea of establishing national unity first. Chiang left Xi'an briefly to coordinate the efforts of other units and of the air force for the campaign. He returned to Xi'an on December 7, and ordered an attack on the Communists for December 12.

The result was one of the most bizarre incidents in

In 1936 in Xi'an, Chiang (right) planned with Marshal
Zhang Xueliang (left) another campaign against the
Communists. But Zhang and his men mutinied, held Chiang
captive, and forced him to agree to form a United Front
with the Communists to fight the Japanese invaders.

Chiang's career, known ever since as the Xi'an Incident.

On December 12, Chiang got up early, as was his custom. As he was shaving, a group of the Young Marshal's soldiers entered his quarters and put him under arrest. This was clearly mutiny—a marshal daring to lay hands on his generalissimo.

The Young Marshal dispatched a telegram to the government in Nanking. It contained, in effect, the ransom demands of a kidnapper: Include the Communists in the government, stop the civil war against them, and resist Japan.

China and the world were stunned. This was 1936. Kidnapping was no longer considered an instrument of international diplomacy. Even in Moscow, where Chiang had been viewed as an arch-enemy, the leaders of world Communist strategy were nonplussed by such direct action.

Some of the mutineers favored killing Chiang at once. But the Communists disagreed with them. Chiang was still the most powerful leader in China. It would be far better if he would agree to stop fighting Communism and fight the Japanese. For the Communists saw that their greatest threat was Japanese expansion in Asia.

As a result of this political analysis of the situation, the Communists resolved to try to save the life of their old enemy. The man they sent to Xi'an for that purpose, Zhou Enlai, had seen thousands of his associates killed by Chiang's soldiers in Shanghai in 1927, but he carried out his new orders well.

By Christmas Day, Chiang had agreed to the policy reversal his captors demanded. The Young Marshal then publicly confessed he had made a mistake, and accompanied Chiang back to the capital in Nanking. He was sentenced to ten years in prison, but was granted amnesty.

During the first half of 1937, the Communists and the Nationalists laid plans for a United Front against the Japanese. Those plans were carefully watched in Japan where the military leaders resolved to strike before Chiang grew any stronger. On July 7, 1937, the Japanese army, without orders from the government, provoked an incident near Peking that plunged China and Japan into a full-fledged war.

mong the many rights that had been exacted by foreign nations from the tottering Manchu Dynasty in the nineteenth century was the right to station troops in China. In 1937, Japanese troops protected the rail line from Peking to the port of Tianjin, a line operated by a Japanese company.

On July 7, 1937, the commander of these Japanese troops told the Chinese officer in charge in the village of Wanbing (just north of Peking) that one of his soldiers was missing, and demanded permission to search for him in the village. The Chinese commander refused, an argument ensued, a shot was fired. A short skirmish between Chinese and Japanese soldiers followed near a bridge known as the Marco Polo Bridge. It was clear the whole incident was manufactured by the Japanese army leaders to give them an excuse for military action against China. It was also clear that they did not care whether anyone accepted that excuse—they were determined to invade China. Japanese troops began to pour across the border from Manchuria.

The invasion drew the Chinese people together and

EIGHT

The War Against Japan

gave them greater unity than they had known for many decades. In 1937 and 1938, there really was a United Front against the Japanese.

Nevertheless in the first months of the war, China's armies were no match for the highly organized, well-equipped soldiers of Japan. On July 28, Chiang ordered the evacuation of Peking to protect its historic treasures from war's destruction. Tianjin also fell. Chiang adopted a strategy expressed as "trading land for time." Since China is a huge country, he would let the Japanese occupy part of it, while he grouped his armies for a strong defense.

That strong defense began in August, 1937, when the Japanese landed more troops near the mouth of the Yangtze River, in an effort to take the great port of Shanghai. Chiang sent his best troops to the defense of that city and the Japanese were halted. For three months the defense held. Chinese casualties were heavy, but Chiang kept pouring in reinforcements. The defense of Shanghai gave a powerful boost to national morale, for it showed the Japanese were not invincible. And it aroused admiration around the world for Chiang and for China.

In December the Japanese landed additional troops

behind Chiang's defense lines, and captured Shanghai. Then they advanced rapidly to the capital, Nanking. Chiang saw it was hopeless to defend that city, so he resolved to move his government to the interior of China. Japanese tanks and mechanized units had swept easily across the flat plains of eastern China. But they would be useless in the mountainous western part of the country, where the only means of transportation were small boats on the swift rivers and human labor carrying loads along narrow footpaths. In an amazing show of national determination, the Chinese used those rivers and those footpaths to move their capital to the city of Chongqing in Sichuan province, where the Yangtze rushes through narrow mountain gorges. Government workers loaded whatever was movable in their offices onto boats, and set off themselves on foot for Chongqing. University students and professors packed up books and laboratories and followed them. Factory owners and workers dismantled their machinery and reassembled it several months later in Chongqing. The patriotic spirit of this great move to the west made these months the high point of Chiang's career.

The Japanese were furious. They had expected the capture of the capital at Nanking to mark the end of Chinese resistance. The Japanese commanders lost control of their soldiers, who went on a rampage through Nanking that resulted in the death of 100,000 civilians. Their "Rape of Nanking" ranks among the blackest pages of the history of the twentieth century.

During the three months that Chiang's lines held along the Yangtze near Shanghai, the Japanese troops in North China had been capturing province after province. After Shanghai and Nanking fell, the commanders in the north attempted to link up with the commanders in the Yangtze

Valley, to capture the important communications junction of Suzhou. Here the Chinese again offered stiff resistance, and held Suzhou until May 19, 1938.

The next major Japanese objective was the industrial center of Wuhan, on the Yangtze, 500 miles upriver from Shanghai. In order to slow the advance of the Japanese from the north, the Chinese opened the dikes that contained the Yellow River as it flowed across the coastal plain to the sea. The resulting flood played havoc with Japanese strategy, as intended, but it also drowned thousands of Chinese civilians and destroyed the livelihood of millions more. It was the ultimate example of "trading land for time."

In October, 1938, the Japanese launched another invasion in the south and captured Canton. That same month Wuhan fell. The Japanese were now in control in every major city in China. But the military situation had reached a stalemate. The Chinese government was firmly established inland in Chongqing, and showed no inclination to surrender.

And while all of the eastern part of the country was occupied by Japanese troops, the several hundred million people who lived there were still loyal to Chiang. That fact thwarted Japan's intention to use China as a land base for additional conquests on the mainland of Asia. Most important of all, as it turned out, the northwest corner of China was still under the control of the Chinese Communists.

The outcome of the Chinese-Japanese conflict depended less on the military situation in China than on international developments. The military now ruled Japan, in cooperation with the nation's major industrialists. In Europe, similar coalitions ruled in Nazi Germany and Fascist Italy. In 1936, Japan had signed an Anti-Commintern pact with Germany creating a "Rome-Berlin-Tokyo Axis" whose ostensible purpose was opposition to world Communism. Germany proceeded to demonstrate this "opposition" by invading Austria in 1938, and Czechoslovakia and Poland in 1939. The invasion caused Britain and France to declare war on Germany. Japan announced as her objective the establishment of a "Greater East Asia Co-Prosperity Sphere," under Japanese leadership, and set out to drive the British from their colonies in Burma and Malaya, the French from Vietnam, Laos and Cambodia, and the Dutch from the islands of the East Indies.

Chiang was confident that eventually Axis aggression would bring the Soviet Union or the United States into the widening war. Then he would have all the help he needed against the Japanese. In the meantime, his best course, he felt, was to conserve the strength of his troops, and wait.

The United Front of Chiang's Nationalists, and the Chinese Communists was still talked about by both parties, and the Communists practiced guerrilla warfare against the Japanese, using tactics they knew well. For the first time since Chiang's rise to power, the Communists were free from Nationalist attack. Mao Zedong saw in the situation an opportunity to enlist the support of the Chinese people. He set up additional soviet governments in the provinces of north China, winning support of the masses by offering them land reform and the opportunity to fight in a well-disciplined army against the Japanese.

Chiang was well aware of what Mao was doing. The Communist units were supposedly under Chiang's command in the United Front. But when he ordered the Communists to move their New Fourth Army from its position near Shanghai, they refused. Obviously, they hoped to control that vital port, once the war with Japan was over.

Lt. Gen. Joseph W. Stilwell, right, commanded U.S. forces in China in World War II. His acid speech earned him the nickname "Vinegar Joe," but he had a deep concern for the welfare of his troops and shared their hardships in the field.

Chiang sent Nationalist troops to enforce his order. A major clash occurred on January 5, 1941, and that was the end of the United Front.

Chiang's expectations of the widening of the war soon came true. In June, 1941, Hitler invaded the Soviet Union. And on December 7, 1941, Japanese planes attacked United States naval bases in the Pacific, including the one in Hawaii at Pearl Harbor. The United States at once declared war against Japan and Germany. Chiang had a strong ally at last.

The alliance immediately ran into two serious problems. The first was purely physical—how could the United States get help to Chiang, far in the interior of China.

Only one route to Chongqing was not in Japanese hands: by rail across Burma from the port of Rangoon to the end of the line at Lashio, and from there by road to China. The United States asked permission to send supplies through the Soviet Union to Chiang's troops in North China, but the Soviet refused on the grounds that the supplies might be used by Chiang against the Chinese Communists.

That fear was not without foundation. For the second serious problem of the American-Chinese alliance concerned long-range strategy. The Americans wanted to strengthen all the armies in China so that they could fight against Japan. Chiang wanted aid to go only to his Nationalist armies.

The American assigned to deal with these two problems was Lt. General Joseph W. Stilwell. General Stilwell was a brilliant military strategist. He also had more knowledge of China than any other American officer. He had served many years as military attaché at the American Embassy, had learned to speak Chinese, and had traveled extensively in the country—often on foot when no other transportation was available.

Stilwell detested all protocol and pretension and in the field he regularly shared the hardships of his men. He had a great conviction that wars are won by the troops, not by the generals, and he worked throughout his career to see to it that his troops were well trained, well led and well cared for. Stilwell expected Chiang to do the same for China's soldiers, whom he had observed often in his travels. Once he wrote, "I believe the Chinese soldier to be the equal of any in the world, given the proper leadership." In January, 1942, Stilwell was appointed commander of all the Allied forces in China and also Chief of Staff under Chiang Kaishek.

The Burma Road, cut through mountains nine thousand feet high, was the only land route available for sending supplies to China's armies, after the Japanese captured all her ports. This section of the road doubles back on itself twenty-two times.

Stilwell was primarily a soldier, not a diplomat. He turned his attention first to the military situation in Burma, when the Japanese invasion begun in December, 1941, threatened to cut Chiang's last land route to the outside world—the Burma Road. He stepped up the training program of the best Chinese regiments, and hoped that their aid would enable the British troops in Burma to stop the Japanese advance.

Stilwell personally led the Chinese troops into Burma, but the Japanese were too strong for them. Stilwell said, with characteristic candor, that the Allies took a beating. On February 25, 1942, the Japanese cut the Burma Road.

The airplane was the only means of transportation left that could carry supplies to Chiang. The Allies set up a regular air cargo service from India over "the Hump," that is, over the Himalaya. It was the most dangerous flying in the world. The example of courage and determination set by these pilots made a tremendous contribution to the war effort, out of all proportion to the actual quantity of supplies they could carry.

Since 1940, a group of American volunteer pilots, known as the Flying Tigers, had been active in China. Their leader, Brig. General Claire L. Chennault, firmly believed that air power could win the war in Asia. While Stilwell was advising Chiang to strengthen his foot soldiers for long hard ground fighting, Chennault was promising that bombers based in China could raid Japan's home islands and end the conflict.

In the first year of the Alliance, then, Stilwell's two problems both worsened. Getting supplies to China was more difficult than ever. And persuading Chiang to reunite with the Communists against the Japanese was more difficult also. A large part of the Nationalists' best troops had been lost in the fighting in Burma. Chiang was determined not to lose any more of his strength. He saw that once the war with Japan was over, he would still have to fight the Communists. He intended to be ready for that day.

Viewed from the standpoint of the interests of the Nationalist Party, or from the viewpoint of opposing Communism, Chiang's position made sense. He was sincerely convinced that the future good of China depended on the success of his party. All other considerations were secondary, he felt. And there, he was wrong.

While Chiang himself was incorruptible, many of his subordinates were not. Both his army and his government were staffed by men more interested in accumulating wealth than in building China's strength. Army commanders received lump sums of money to run their armies. Any money that was left over after they paid and fed their troops was theirs to keep. That system created a great temptation to use minimum amounts for the soldiers. Conditions in the armies were pathetic, with the men often sick and on the border of starvation. Each year thousands died before they ever saw action against the enemy; and thousands of new recruits were rounded up by force to take their places. Chiang issued stern orders forbidding such abuse, but did not enforce the orders.

Nationalist officials were responsible for administering the money and supplies that came to China from the United States. But they were not required to give a careful accounting of their actions. Many sold the supplies and pocketed the money. In addition, Chongqing maintained a lively trade with the Japanese in Shanghai.

The contrast between conditions in Chongqing and in the Communist Northwest was inescapable. Mao Zedong continued his policy of winning the support of the ordinary people. Communist soldiers fought for a cause they believed in, under leaders they respected. And for the first time farmers in the Communist-dominated areas got a fair share of the food they grew, thanks to the land reform program.

Between the Nationalists and the Communists there still existed a number of middle-of-the-road parties. They had had no say in the government for many years. A democratic National Assembly had been elected in 1936, but Chiang had established a virtual dictatorship of the Nationalist Party to deal with the Japanese invasion. Now the intellectuals of China began to call for a government that would represent all the parties, including the Communists. Chiang replied that the middle of a war was no time to try a new form of government. It was a logical answer. But corruption continued, and discontent with the Nationalists grew among the intellectuals. And their support was necessary for the continued functioning of any government.

Meanwhile, in Washington and London, President Franklin D. Roosevelt and Prime Minister Winston Churchill received reports month by month of the problems of having Chiang as an ally. They had treated him as an equal partner early in the war, as a member of the "Big Four"—Britain, China, the Soviet Union and the United

In December 1943, Chiang Kaishek, accompanied by Madame Chiang, traveled to Cairo to discuss war strategy and postwar objectives with U.S. President Franklin D. Roosevelt (second left) and British Prime Minister Winston S. Churchill.

States. That status recognized Chinese resistance to Japan since 1937. But now Chiang demanded more and more weapons, more and more money and an Allied seaborne invasion to recapture Burma. At the same time he refused to commit his own troops to a land offensive in Burma proposed by Stilwell, and he refused to allow Stilwell to use the Communist troops. Instead, he maintained a blockade of the Northwest which not only ruled out major Communist participation in the war, but also immobilized 400,000 Nationalist troops.

Stilwell's frustration grew. The corruption he saw disgusted him, and he repeatedly called on Chiang to correct it. Furthermore Chiang's hoarding of his men and supplies was making it impossible for Stilwell to carry out his military mission. Stilwell was an outspoken man. His acid tongue had early earned him the nickname "Vinegar Joe." His meetings with Chiang grew more and more acrimonious. In his diary, he regularly referred to Chiang as "The Peanut." And in his dispatches to Washington, he minced no words in his criticisms of Chinese leadership. Gradually President Roosevelt began to acknowledge the validity of those criticisms.

At that point Chiang was making two main contributions to the war. Occupation of the country kept a large part of Japan's army out of the fighting elsewhere in Asia. And air bases in China allowed the Flying Tigers to bomb Japanese cities. For the sake of those contributions, Roosevelt tried to maintain good relations with Chiang. All through 1943, dispatches flew back and forth between Chongqing and Washington. Plans were proposed and rejected. Criticisms were met with countercriticisms.

In 1944, the Allies began to drive the Japanese out of the islands they had captured in the South Pacific. D-Day saw the invasion of the continent of Europe. The tide of war turned against the Axis.

Stilwell warned that the Japanese would try to capture the air bases in China, to stop the bombing of Japan. He urged Chiang to strengthen the defense of the bases, but Chiang ignored the danger. The Japanese proved Stilwell right, and captured not only the bases but also huge quantities of supplies that had been airlifted at great cost on the dangerous route over the Hump. It was the last major Japanese military action in China.

Roosevelt sent a series of high-ranking representatives to China to try to achieve cooperation between Chiang and Stilwell. But by that time the animosity between the two strong-willed men had grown too great. Chiang demanded that Stilwell be removed as commander. Roosevelt, hoping that a more diplomatic general would have more success with Chiang, replaced Stilwell in October, 1944.

By that time Chiang and Mao Zedong were both thinking almost entirely of the question of who would rule China after Japan was defeated and her troops withdrawn. Roosevelt was thinking of that too, and his representatives visited Mao as well as Chiang. They were frankly surprised by what they saw in the Communist-held part of China, and reported that Mao and his followers seemed to be agrarian reformers sincerely interested in improving the lot of the Chinese people. Favorable reports on the Communists, coupled with disillusionment with the Nationalists, led American leaders to believe that the best course for China would be establishment of a government in which both parties were represented. Consequently the Americans persuaded Chiang and Mao to declare a truce, and begin negotiations on the form such a government might take. The negotiations continued for months, but each party demanded a structure that would ensure its maximum strength.

The war was going well in Europe. In the Pacific, the Allies were also winning, but the Japanese soldiers fought with a kind of religious fanaticism. Their ancient code "Death before Dishonor" meant that they never surrendered, no matter what the odds against them. On island after island, Japanese commanders and individual soldiers followed that code to the letter. Reconquest of the Pacific meant killing or capturing every Japanese unit. It promised to be a slow and costly victory for the Allies.

Since Chiang was providing so little help in the actual fighting, the Allies sought to bring the Soviet Union into the war against Japan. The Soviets had declared war on Germany when Hitler's armies invaded their territory, but had not declared war on Japan. In February, 1945, Stalin met with Roosevelt and Churchill at Yalta, a Russian beach resort. He drove a hard bargain. As the price of providing help against Japan, beginning two or three months after the defeat of Germany, he obtained the promise of control of the major railways in Manchuria. The promise simply ratified the military facts in that year —Manchuria had been occupied by the Japanese since 1931. Should Japan surrender, the Allied army nearest to Manchuria was Stalin's, just across the Amur River. The next nearest army was Mao Zedong's in Northwest China.

Events moved swiftly after that. In April, 1945, President Roosevelt died and Vice President Harry S Truman became president. In May, with Allied armies approaching Berlin, Hitler committed suicide and Germany surrendered. On July 16, Allied physicists carried out the first successful test of an atomic bomb—the weapon that was to bring a sudden end to the war in the Pacific. President Truman determined that victory over Japan in island-by-island fighting might cost an additional 200,000 American lives. Japanese casualties would be even higher. On July 26, an Allied declaration called on the Japanese to surrender to avoid that loss of life, and warned that if they refused they faced "prompt and utter destruction." Allied planes dropped leaflets on Japan repeating this warning.

The Japanese made no reply, and on August 6, an American bomber dropped an atomic bomb on the port of Hiroshima. Nagasaki followed Hiroshima on August 9, and on August 14, Japan surrendered unconditionally to the Allies.

The end of the war had come sooner than anyone had expected. Jubilation and relief swept over the United States. Now the soldiers would come home and the world would be at peace, Americans believed. The Allies had already formed the United Nations Organization to maintain that peace.

The Chinese had less confidence in orderly procedures in a peaceful future. Even before Chiang announced the surrender over Chongqing radio, he gave orders to Communist Commander-in-Chief Zhu De forbidding him to move his troops. Zhu ignored the orders and sent his soldiers racing across North China to get possession of the weapons of the defeated Japanese. And Stalin moved his armies across the Amur River into Manchuria, to claim his payment.

anchuria, the northeast corner of China, is rich in iron and coal. That natural wealth gives it a great attraction for any ruler seeking to build an industrial nation in East Asia. According to Chiang Kaishek, possession of Manchuria was the whole reason for the war between China and Japan. But in 1945, that war ended sooner than anyone expected. Chiang saw that the prize might be taken from him.

In August, the Chinese Communist armies moved into Manchuria from the south, and the armies of the Soviet Union moved in from the north. Chiang's own best troops were thousands of miles away, in Southwest China and in Burma. To deal with this situation, General Douglas Mac-Arthur, Supreme Commander of the Allied Powers, made American ships and planes available to Chiang for the transport of his soldiers. He also directed the defeated Japanese commanders in China and Manchuria to surrender only to Chiang's forces. On August 14, the day of the Japanese surrender, Chiang signed a pact with the Soviet Union which he believed guaranteed that the Soviet troops

Mao's Victory

would simply hold the area until the Nationalists got there.

It was clear that the loser in the war in the Pacific was Japan. It was less clear who was the victor. The announced policy of the United States at the war's end was to assist the legitimate government of China in receiving occupied territory back from the Japanese, and to avoid involvement in China's civil strife. The two objectives were contradictory, since the "legitimate government" meant the Nationalists until a new government of all parties could be formed.

American advisers urged the Chinese to proceed quickly to the formation of such a government. Because Chiang needed American support, he could not reject that idea out of hand. He invited Mao to come to Chongqing for a conference. Mao hesitated, but when United States Ambassador Patrick J. Hurley offered to escort him personally to Chongqing, and guaranteed his safety, he accepted the invitation and went to the capital on August 28. Nevertheless Chiang and Mao both continued moving troops into Manchuria. Seven years before, Mao had said, "Political power grows from the barrel of a gun." That summed up concisely the belief of both men. Their conference served to identify various areas of disagreement over a new government for China. Most important, Mao wanted Communist troops to make up a certain proportion of the new government's army, and Mao wanted the right to appoint the governors of a number of provinces. The Conference broke up in November.

By November, Manchuria was occupied by four different armies. The Japanese were still there, waiting for Chiang's men to come and accept their surrender. The airlift provided by General MacArthur had enabled Chiang to occupy a few inland cities. Mao had 130,000 troops there. And the Russians were there, as they had promised to be.

Chiang soon learned that Stalin was a doubtful ally. When Nationalist troops on American ships arrived at the Manchurian port of Dairen, Soviet troops refused to allow them to land. At two other ports, Mao's men blocked the way. The ships finally docked just south of the Great Wall —the ancient boundary between Manchuria and North China.

At that point Chiang knew if he wanted Manchuria he still had to fight for it. His American military advisers warned him not to attempt action there until he had consolidated his strength in China proper, and established adequate supply lines. But Chiang always thought his strategy was best, and on November 15, he sent an army across the Great Wall. He simply could not believe that Mao's peasant recruits could match the strength of his best regiments, armed with American weapons and trained by American officers to fight the Japanese. And he expected that aid from the United States would continue.

For a few weeks it seemed that Chiang's confidence was justified. The Communists withdrew before the advancing Nationalists, offering only light resistance. But the future was to be determined by factors far more complex than raw military strength. Chiang was losing support both in China and in the world.

The Chinese people had been at war longer than any other participants in World War II. Now Chiang was asking them to fight again, against other Chinese. Moreover, he was asking them to fight for a government that, week by week, was proving itself unworthy of support. In city after city, Nationalist officials arrived at the end of the war to take control from the Japanese armies of occupation.

Clerks collect their small pay in large bundles of banknotes as a result of disastrous inflation after World War II. Inflation and corruption soon caused the people to lose all confidence in the government of Chiang Kaishek.

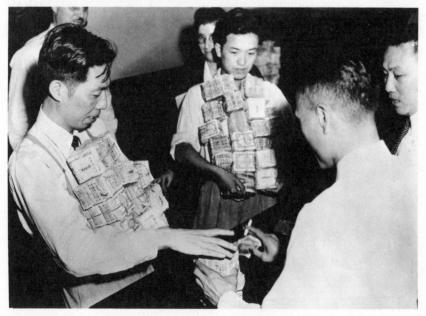

The chief result was to spread the corruption that had so disgusted Stilwell in Chongqing. The national government exercised little control. Its finances were a shambles. To pay its bills it resorted to the classic remedy of weak governments, the printing of more and more paper money. Disastrous inflation followed throughout China, wiping out whatever savings the people had managed to hold onto during the war. Only the officials prospered. Millions of Chinese remembered the stories they had heard about the Communist armies on the Long March: how the soldiers had dealt honestly with the peasants, and how their leaders had promised fair distribution of farmland— the only wealth a family could depend on. Could the Communists be any worse than these greedy Nationalists?

Chiang's international allies were asking the same question—when they were forced to think about China at all. The Big Four alliance of Britain, China, the Soviet Union and the United States had been held together by the need to fight common enemies. Now that those enemies were defeated, each nation naturally turned to building its own future. The war had put an end to colonialism of the type practiced in the nineteenth century. British, French and Dutch colonies in Southeast Asia had been captured by the Japanese, liberated by the Allies, and now were claiming status as independent nations. The British Empire was ended; the British Commonwealth of Nations had the task of working out a new relationship to give greater independence to each of the member nations. For China, the end of colonialism meant the end of all the foreign demands for treaty rights, concessions, extraterritoriality and other infringements on her sovereignty. The formal ending of the last of the "unequal treaties" in 1943 would have been a cause for rejoicing, had China time to notice it.

Two members of the Big Four, the United States and the Soviet Union, emerged from the war as the strongest nations in the world. The two "superpowers," journalists named them. They had been wartime allies, but it was difficult for them to be peacetime partners, because of their differences in ideology—differences in their understanding of the proper relationship between man and government. The difficulties between the superpowers immediately had an effect on China. This was most evident in their reactions to Chiang's decision in November, 1945, to fight for control of Manchuria.

The Soviets were reluctant to have Manchuria fall into the hands of such a lifelong foe of Communism as Chiang, and delayed withdrawing their troops. The Americans wanted Manchuria to be controlled by the new representative government of China that they had been working for since 1943. Accordingly, President Truman dispatched to China a man respected throughout the world, General of the Army George C. Marshall. Marshall had been Chief of Staff of all American forces in the war, and had earned the title "architect of the victory." The President told him: "I desire that you endeavor to persuade the Chinese Government to call a national conference of representatives of the major political elements to bring about the unification of China and, concurrently, to effect a cessation of hostilities, particularly in North China." If anybody could accomplish that, Marshall could.

Marshall arrived in China in mid-December, 1945, four weeks after Chiang had sent his troops into Manchuria. He spent the next year patiently working at his assignment. Largely by his personal prestige he got the Communists and the Nationalists to sit down at the conference table again, and to agree to a temporary truce. But the old problem remained: neither side would trust a new government enough to give up any military strength. So 1946 saw an alternation of talking and fighting, with the fighting becoming more and more dominant month by month.

By March, 1946, Stalin was ready to keep the promise to turn Manchuria over to the Nationalists, and withdraw his troops. But Communists and Nationalists both learned with dismay that those troops were taking home with them a large part of the heavy machinery of Manchuria's factories. "War compensation" they called it. The money needed to replace the industrial equipment they shipped out has been estimated at close to two billion dollars.

Furthermore, while Stalin's troops in southern Manchuria turned over to Chiang's men control of the major cities and of the railroads, the population of the countryside largely supported Mao. Chinese Communist recruiting teams had continued their work of enlisting party members. And among the new members were thousands of Manchurians who had been given military training by the Japanese. Quantities of Japanese weapons and ammunition were seized by the Chinese Communists before they could be turned over to Chiang—if indeed that had ever been Stalin's intention.

On March 5, 1946, Chiang's troops peacefully occupied Shenyang, the capital of Manchuria, three days after Stalin's troops left. On March 17, Mao's armies went into action. Since November, they had given little opposition to Chiang's advance northward into Manchuria. That advance had proceeded rapidly thanks to control of the railways, and the assistance of American air transport. Now in March, Mao's men attacked and captured a strategic rail junction, Sibing, north of Shenyang. They held it for two crucial months while Stalin's forces were withdrawing from northern Manchuria. Their blockade allowed the Communists rather than the Nationalists to occupy the territory the Russians left. When Chiang's men finally recaptured the junction on May 20, Mao was firmly in control of the north.

Mao's strategy now became evident. In late May, he attacked at several points in South Manchuria and North China. Despite the warnings of American advisers, Chiang had committed his best troops to Manchuria, confident of victory. Mao intended to bottle up those troops. It was a simple, obvious strategy. Chiang simply did not believe the Communists were strong enough to carry it out.

Perhaps Chiang was right, by a strict military count of men and weapons. But he failed to realize the extent to which the Nationalist government had lost the support of the people. In one of the battles in May, a Nationalist division switched over to the Communist side. It was the beginning of a long, slow collapse of Chiang's power.

In June, Marshall achieved another truce, and reopened discussions between Nationalists and Communists. But it was now apparent that the objectives of the two sides were irreconcilable. Neither side would agree to conditions proposed by the other. On June 30, the truce expired, and fighting resumed. Marshall continued his efforts for peace until January 1947, when he returned to the United States to become Secretary of State. In his summation of his mission to China, he wrote, "In the first place, the greatest obstacle to peace has been the complete, almost overwhelming suspicion with which the Chinese Communist party and the Guomindang (Nationalist Party) regard each other." Reactionaries in the Nationalist party were working against a coalition government, he continued. And the "dyed-in-the-wool Communists" in Mao's ranks were willing

to wreck the entire economy to achieve their ends. "The salvation of the situation, as I see it," Marshall wrote, "would be the assumption of leadership by the liberals in the Government and in the minority parties, a splendid group of men, but who as yet lack the political power to exercise a controlling influence."

In the summer and fall of 1946, Chiang continued occupying more and more towns in Manchuria, which meant his troops were spread thinner and thinner, and his supply lines were stretched longer and longer. His generals kept trying for a decisive battle with the Communists, but Mao's units would fight for a while and then withdraw to preserve their strength. As winter approached, the Nationalists paused to consolidate their gains and prepare for a big push the following spring on North Manchuria.

Now Mao again took the initiative. In January, 1947, he began a series of attacks in various sectors, testing Nationalist strength. Month by month these attacks grew stronger and drove farther south. When the offensive ended in June, the Nationalists retained control of the major cities, but the Communist drives had wrecked the rail lines connecting them. Chiang's best troops were isolated from each other, and far from home base.

Chiang sent reinforcements to Manchuria, and replaced a number of generals. But since he insisted on personal control of all military action, even the best generals could do little to improve the situation. Now there

Mao Zedong and his wife, Jiang Qing, ride with Communist troops in 1947. The civil war between the Communists and the Nationalist government of Chiang Kaishek resumed almost as soon as World War II ended.

were almost no Nationalist troops left in central China. And Communist strength there kept growing.

In July President Truman sent a new mission to China to analyze the situation. Chiang still believed the United States would provide whatever aid was necessary to prevent defeat of the Nationalists. The Americans turned over to him surplus supplies, ammunition, weapons, even planes and ships. As one American military observer expressed it, no battle was lost for want of men or materiel. It was leadership that was lacking. The Congress questioned the wisdom of pouring more money into China, when it yielded such poor results. A figure of 300 million dollars in additional aid was discussed in Washington, to which the Nationalists replied that 3 billion dollars would be more like what was needed. Madame Chiang flew to Washington to use her great charm to obtain more help but to no avail. The only American action that might prevent Communist domination in China was a massive commitment of American troops, led by American generals. No one could calculate the cost of such an effort, or its chances of success. It was a commitment the American people were not prepared to make.

All over China, citizens felt the ruinous effects of the Nationalists' economic policy, or lack of policy. Inflation proceeded so rapidly that prices in 1947 were four million times what they were in 1937. It took a basketful of money to buy a handful of rice. Even the Chinese capitalists, their fortunes wrecked, turned against Chiang and his government.

In September, 1947, Mao launched another offensive aimed at isolating Manchuria completely. Geography favored him, for the only land route to China crosses a narrow neck of land bordered on the east by the sea and on the west by the Jehol Mountains. By blocking this corridor,

Mao could prevent reinforcements from coming in, and Chiang's armies from getting out. He would have them in the trap he had been planning for two years.

It took many months of hard fighting to effect that blockade. Winter came on again, but fighting continued, with the Communists winning more and more often. In Nanking the United States Army still maintained an advisory group. Major General David Barr advised Chiang in March, 1948, to get his armies out of Manchuria while he still could. Chiang refused to consider such an idea. But his weakness in China proper was underlined when Communist armies in several provinces captured key cities.

Slowly the trap closed. Mao gradually encircled the Manchurian cities held by the Nationalists. By September Chiang saw he could not hold Manchuria, but it was too late to evacuate his men. Only a few thousand escaped by ship. One entire army and part of another went over to the Communist side. All the others surrendered, along with huge quantities of their weapons and supplies.

In all, the Manchurian campaign lost Chiang 400,000 men, and those the elite of his army.

Two days after the Nationalists surrendered in Manchuria, Mao began the battle for China itself, and the capital at Nanking. Chiang chose to draw his line of defense about 150 miles north of the capital, on the plains between the Longhai railroad and the Huai River. Here he sent into battle a unit he had held back all this time to protect Nanking: his Armored Corps of tanks and mobile weapons, commanded by his own son, Chiang Weiguo. The plains were well suited to tank warfare, and perhaps that was why Chiang chose to fight there, rejecting his commanders' urgent recommendations that the Huai River was the natural defense line.

The Battle of the Huai-Hai, as it is called, began on

November 7, and lasted for sixty-five days. Once again Mao simply cut off all the Nationalists' lines of communications, and surrounded their armies. When the Armored Corps tried to break through the encirclement, its way was blocked by deep trenches Mao's men had prepared for it. Too late the Corps learned that the Communists now had American heavy weapons too, as artillery captured from the Nationalists blasted away at them. After six weeks of fighting, three-quarters of the half million men Chiang had committed to the battle had been lost. The remaining quarter had been pushed into an area of six square miles, along with their tanks. Rather than lose those tanks to the enemy, Nanking Headquarters proposed to send bombing planes to destroy them. At that news, the encircled men surrendered, and the battle ended January 12, 1949.

Nationalist commanders in Peking and Tianjin capitulated that same month. In all Chiang had lost more than half of his troop strength between September, 1948, and January, 1949—a million and a half men dead, wounded, surrendered or gone over to the Communist side. He made a vain appeal to the United States, Britain, France, and the Soviet Union for help.

The Communists entered Nanking on April 22. After that they took city after city, province after province, meeting only slight opposition.

Seeing that defeat was inevitable, Chiang moved his government from city to city, and finally in December to the island of Taiwan, 100 miles off the southeast coast of China. With him went the government's stock of gold, and about a million citizens, both soldiers and civilians. Chiang planned to make of the island a fortress for continuing the struggle.

On October 1, 1949, Mao established at Peking the

Central People's Government of the People's Republic of China. The Communists viewed their victory as the culmination of a social revolution that began a century before with the Taiping Rebellion. They controlled China at last. Now they would have to prove they could rule it.

he Chinese people have stood up. Never again will the Chinese be an enslaved people." Mao Zedong spoke those words the day of the establishment of the People's Republic of China, October 1, 1949, to an enormous crowd assembled at Tiananmen, the great gate in the wall of the Forbidden City in Peking. Soon ordinary Chinese by the thousands would be trooping inside that wall to see the palaces and temples created for the emperors. The emperors' rule had ended in 1911. The Nationalist Government of Generalissimo Chiang Kaishek had failed to live up to its promise of "new life" for the people, and popular support had turned overwhelmingly to Mao. Now it was his responsibility to provide a government for a nation with more citizens than any other on earth.

The People's Republic of China was the creation of a conference Mao had called in Peking in June, 1949. The conference was dominated, of course, by the new majority party, the Communists. But Mao knew, as had the Mongol and Manchu conquerors before him, that only the staff of the existing Chinese civil service had the experience

TEN

Organizing the 600 Million

necessary to attend to the day-to-day affairs of such a vast country—operating the mails and the banking system and the transportation network and all the rest. And only the owners and managers of plants large and small had the know-how to keep producing cloth and tools and all the other manufactured items the people needed. These men had belonged to the Nationalist and other parties. Since Mao had no choice but to keep them at work, the other parties were also given seats at the conference.

A new government required a new constitution. Writing a constitution takes time, even when one strong leader can squelch every argument about its contents. So the conference adopted an interim program and set of laws for the People's Republic. The actual constitution was adopted in 1954, and revised in 1975. The basic structure has stayed the same, however—a structure modeled on the example of the Soviet Union. A National People's Congress is, in theory, the supreme authority. It meets irregularly, and between meetings its power is delegated to various committees. Government functions are carried out by various departments (Agriculture, Defense, Foreign Affairs etc.).

On October 1, 1949, in Peking's Tiananmen Square, Mao Zedong proclaimed the establishment of a new government, the People's Republic of China.

Heads of the departments make up a council, similar to the Cabinet in the United States and Great Britain, presided over by a premier. From 1949 until his death in 1976, the post of premier was held by China's master of negotiation, Zhou Enlai. The national structure is repeated in twenty-one provinces and at lower levels. Special provision was made for vast areas in China's west, sparsely populated by Mongols and other ethnic groups. These were designated "autonomous regions," that is, self-governing units.

True power in China, however, belongs to the Chinese Communist Party. The Party structure closely resembles the government structure. A large Party Congress, meeting irregularly, delegates authority to a smaller Central Committee, and decisions are really reached by a still smaller Politburo (Political Bureau) made up of only twenty-four members. Mao was Chairman of the Party; the title by which he became known throughout the world was "Chairman Mao."

There is a third element in the power structure of China—the Army. In the United States, the commander in chief of the armed forces is the president, elected by the people. Since 1912, almost from the beginning of republican government in China, its president had been the general who had the most loyal army. Mao had had his difficulties with other leaders of the Chinese Communist Party, especially over how much to follow directions from Moscow. But the People's Liberation Army was led by his comrades of the Long March, with Zhu De holding the post of commander in chief. Its ranks now numbered five million men. Mao divided the nation into six military districts, commanded by six loyal generals. This third element in the government ensured that his military victory over the Nationalists would be consolidated into firm control over the country. Beyond that, it ensured that his plans for a "New China" would be carried out. And for thirty years, members of the army have played a major role in the political and economic life of every community in the land.

For protection against foreign interference in his plans,

Mao needed a strong friend. In December, 1949, he went to Moscow, his first trip abroad, to negotiate a treaty of mutual defense against aggression. Aggression seemed a real possibility, from several quarters.

While Mao was creating a new government in Peking, Chiang Kaishek was busy reinstalling the old government on the island of Taiwan. Chiang had ample experience for the task, having already moved his capital from Peking to Nanking to Chongqing and back to Nanking. Since his rule was a virtual dictatorship, it might be said that anywhere he unpacked his suitcases was the capital. Taiwan had been colonized by the Chinese in the seventeenth century, and won by the Japanese from China in the 1894–1895 war. The Japanese had done much to develop industry and agriculture on the island. Japan's defeat in World War II restored the island to China, as a separate province. Chiang now declared that Taiwan was still a province of China, and its capital, Taibei, was now the new capital of the nation. The circumstance that 99.7% of the nation's territory was controlled by Communist bandits was only temporary, he said, and he would soon recapture it from them.

More than a million Chinese followed Chiang to Taiwan, bringing the island population to 15 million. Since many of the newcomers were leading business and government figures, and they brought with them most of the nation's gold reserves, they were soon able to dominate the life of the island. (It should be noted, however, that three key men were missing: T. V. Soong, H. H. Kung and Chen Lifu, the heads of three of China's four most influential families, the fourth being Chiang's own. Those three had decided to take up residence in the United States.) The influx of skills and capital provided a strong stimulus to the growth of the island's economy. In the years ahead, trade with the United States and with Japan increased many times, per capita income rose, and Taiwan achieved one of

Chiang Kaishek reviews his troops on the island of Taiwan, where he and a million other Chinese fled after the Communists' victory on the mainland.

the highest standards of living in Asia. Still, there were limits to the island's strength. Chiang based his hopes for returning to the mainland on the possibility of massive help from the United States. If that was refused him, might not a Third World War set capitalists against communists and defeat bandit chief Mao, the same way the Japanese conquest of China was ended by the Second World War?

President Truman still had no intention of participating in a war on the continent of Asia. However he and his advisers did see a need for maintaining a string of island bases in the Pacific, stretching from Japan to the Philippines. Taiwan was a link in the chain. He began to send large quantities of economic and military aid to build up Chiang's strength. In 1954, the U.S. signed a treaty with Chiang providing for mutual defense. Since governments change, leaders die, national interests alter, most treaties contain an escape clause. This one provided that the treaty could be terminated by either side giving the other a year's notice. At that point, Mao had a mutual defense treaty with one superpower, the Soviet Union, and Chiang had one with the other.

Chiang had one further advantage. As one of the Big Four allies fighting World War II, China had been awarded a seat on the Security Council of the United Nations. Mao said that the People's Republic was now the legitimate government of China, and therefore its representative should take the Chinese seat. While many nations supported him in this view, it was years before he could gather enough votes to bring about the change.

The Nationalist army on Taiwan was only one of several military worries Mao had. In three places where China borders on other nations there was trouble in view. The situation in Korea was the most alarming. The Korean peninsula juts down from China's northeast corner, Manchuria, where most of her industry is located. North and east of Manchuria is the Soviet Union. Korea had been under Japanese control since 1910, and Japanese troops were still there at the end of World War II. After the Japanese surrender, Soviet and American troops occupied the northern and southern halves of the peninsula. Separate governments in North Korea and South Korea resulted—one Communist, the other not—each claiming the right to rule all Korea. In 1949, the United States removed its troops; on June 25, 1950, North Korean forces invaded South Korea.

The United Nations protested this act of aggression, and when the invasion continued, called on United Nations members to send troops for an international force to aid South Korea. Sixteen nations did so, and forty-one others sent supplies. It was the first proof of the United Nations' effectiveness. The United States sent a total of almost half a million men, by far the largest number, almost equal to the 590,000 South Koreans fighting. Under the command of American General Douglas MacArthur, the United Nations forces drove the invaders out of South Korea by the end of September. When MacArthur's demand for surrender was rejected, the United Nations forces crossed into North Korea, capturing its capital, Pyongyang, and then advanced toward the Yalu River separating Korea from China. Mao's government protested, and warned several times that further advances would require China to protect her border by intervening in the war. When advances continued, the People's Liberation Army went into action in Korea. While the United Nations forces had more planes and warships and newer weapons, the People's Liberation Army had much greater reserves of manpower. Chinese General Lin Biao used a tactic known as "man sea," sending wave after wave of foot soldiers into battle. In time the total number of Chinese "volunteers" who helped North Koreans totaled well over a million. By January, 1951, the Communists had pushed the United Nations forces back into South Korea and captured its capital, Seoul. The United Nations forces halted the advance just south of the city, and recaptured Seoul on March 14. After that, both sides dug in, and there were no more spectacular advances by either side. This situation frustrated General MacArthur, who called repeatedly for "total victory." He believed he could achieve that by bombing the bases in northeast China that were supplying the Chinese troops. Many people in the United States supported MacArthur's plan; many others opposed any attack on Chinese territory. President Truman decided against MacArthur's proposal, and when the brilliant but headstrong general refused to accept the decision of his commander in chief, the president relieved him of his command.

The two sides began to talk about peace in July, but limited fighting continued for two more years. In July, 1953, terms for a truce were agreed to. The fighting stopped, but the war had caused hundreds of thousands of casualties on both sides, and had greatly affected China's relations with the rest of the world. From China's standpoint, there had been a very real possibility that a superpower, the United States, would drop bombs on China. From the

American standpoint, China, an old friend and ally, had sent troops into battle who had killed American soldiers and deprived the nation of victory for the first time since the War of 1812. Communism now ruled China, and the Korean War made Communism seem a greater danger than ever before. The Cold War had become a hot war, although both sides limited their actions. One specific result was an increase in military aid to Chiang Kaishek on Taiwan.

A second border area offering possible trouble for Mao's new government was Tibet, high in the Himalaya between China and India. Because of its inaccessibility, Tibet had been little affected by changes in the rest of the world. It was still a state ruled by a religious leader, the Dalai Lama. In 1720, the Emperor Kang Xi had conquered the region and declared it a part of China. In the centuries since, Peking's chief interest in Tibet had been to maintain it as a semi-independent "buffer state," which would absorb any attack in that area. But World War II, with the supply flights over "the Hump," had demonstrated that even the Himalaya could be penetrated by war planes. The end of British rule in India in 1947, and the establishment of the new nation of Pakistan, had been followed by appalling violence. The Tibetan monks would never be able to repel a modern invader. In October, 1950, Mao sent the People's Liberation Army to "consolidate" Tibet into China's Southwest Military District. He promised to create another "autonomous region" for the Tibetans, similar to those of their neighbors. Tibetan army units resisted, but were quickly crushed. Tibet appealed to the United Nations for help, but got none. Its government was forced to sign an agreement in May, 1951, recognizing Chinese control of its domestic and foreign affairs, while the autonomous region was being set up. (That was officially proclaimed fourteen years later, in 1965, but little real power was restored to Tibetans.)

A third border area demanded Mao's attention. The West knew it then as French Indochina, a colony of France from the nineteenth century until its conquest by the Japanese in 1940. After World War II, the French attempted to reestablish their rule there, and the United States supported that effort. The people of Indochina, however, wanted to be independent. In their fight against the French, the most effective leadership came from the Communist Party. Mao sent troops to aid the fight against France's renewal of "Western imperialism," and by 1954, the French were forced out. French Indochina was divided into three nations, called once again by their ancient Asiatic names, Laos, Cambodia and Vietnam. And Vietnam, like Korea, was split in half, with North Vietnam Communist, and South Vietnam not. Apparently, North Vietnam seemed to Mao protection enough for that border; at any rate, he sent no more troops into Vietnam. The development of a "New China" needed the best efforts of every Chinese.

"Every Chinese" meant every woman as well as every man. One of the most radical changes of Mao's first year of rule was the granting of equality to women, embodied in the Marriage Act of 1950. The act provided that women had free choice of a husband, and could no longer be sold in marriage by their families. Divorce was easily obtainable when both parties wanted it. Article 8 reads as follows: "Husband and wife are in duty bound to love, respect, assist and look after each other, to live in harmony, to engage in production, to care for the children and to strive jointly for the welfare of the family and for the building up of a new society." On the farms Chinese women had always "engaged in production," working as hard as the men. Now all women were expected to work. If they had small children, community nurseries would care for them.

Public health campaigns directed at the elimination of such carriers of disease as rats and flies yielded good re-

Women work on a construction project to build Mao's New China. Equality for women, guaranteed by the government, means equal rights and equal responsibility to work.

sults. Opium was outlawed, addicts were rehabilitated, peddlers were arrested. Classes in hygiene were held throughout the nation.

Education for all the people, young and old, was emphasized. Only a very small percentage of the population was able to read and write. From 1949 to 1952 the number of students in primary schools rose from 24 million to 51 million, and in secondary schools from 1 million to 2½ million. All the schools taught the principles of Communism in almost every class, no matter what the subject. The educational effort still had a long way to go, for a population estimated by the government at 582 million, but undoubtedly much larger—about four times the population of the United States in 1950.

The runaway inflation of the last years of Nationalist rule had caused great misery for the people, as they saw money they had spent a lifetime saving drop in value until all they had would not buy one good meal. Inflation also weakened the whole economy of the nation. Mao took immediate measures to control China's money, issuing a new currency, regulating loans and credit, and collecting new taxes to balance the government's budget. In less than a year, his efforts had ended inflation.

The most important of all Mao's programs dealt with the land. His chief goal for China had been stated twenty-two years before in his influential essay, "The Peasant Movement in Hunan." Most of the people who worked the land did not own it and paid a huge share of their crop to landlords as rent. Mao called this a "feudal system," and planned to make an equitable distribution of the land among the people. His primary concern for the farmers made Chinese Communism different from that of the Communist International, with a primary concern for

An outstanding student, eleven years old, studies trigonometry at the University of Science and Technology. Education of all the people, young and old, was essential to Mao's goal of modernizing the Chinese economy.

the proletariat, city dwellers who worked for wages. That difference would be the subject of many struggles in years to come.

The Agrarian Reform Law passed in June, 1950, made a start toward Mao's goal. Some 115 million acres of land were taken from the richest landlords, without payment, and divided among 300 million peasants. The tiny farms that resulted were too small for efficient cultivation, but redistribution was only the beginning. Communist party workers, called cadres, were assigned to villages and held meetings with the farmers to talk about farming methods —and about politics. Units of the People's Liberation Army worked on dams, dikes and irrigation projects. Further progress in agriculture required chemical fertilizer, tractors, harvesting machinery—in a word, modernization.

The goal of modernization had a long history in China, stretching back at least as far as the Self-Strengthening Movement of the 1860s. Then Dowager Empress Ci Xi's ministers had exhorted the nation to study Western science, and at the same time follow the ancient ideals of right relationships described by Confucius. For the 1950s, the ideals were to be found in the writings of Chairman Mao. Any area of life could be improved by the proper application of "Mao Zedong Thought."

Not everyone believed that, of course. While Mao had tremendous popular support, there were still many Chinese who resisted Communism. In order to determine who was guilty of not cooperating with the new government, the Communist Party held thousands of "struggle meetings." These were a form of trial, conducted without laws or legal procedure. Communist Party cadres held the meetings in villages, neighborhoods, schools and factories, to win the support of all the people for Mao's program, they said. They gave a glorious description of the New China that was coming, with everyone working together for the common good. Anyone who opposed this great effort must be selfish or acting from evil motives, they said. Then the cadres encouraged the people at the meetings to tell of bitter experiences they had had in the past. Even little children, taught Mao Zedong Thought in school, were listened to as they criticized their parents' politics. Landlords, factory owners, officials, all those called guilty of oppressing the people, were brought before the meetings and asked to tell of their own wrong actions. Those who showed enough shame were allowed to "reform" and take some lowly job in their own communities. The others were sent away to work in labor battalions to "learn from the people," or were executed. As a result of political education in the schools, constant indoctrination lectures at places of work, and the struggle meetings, many Chinese, usually idealistic young people, resolved to work with the party to build the new China. Many more decided to do their day's work, say they supported Mao, and keep their real thoughts to themselves. Some—relatively few—resolved to leave the country. That was a difficult thing to do, since all travel was tightly controlled. In a few years Mao had all China professing belief in communism. Almost all the American businessmen and missionaries in China in 1949 came home.

No one knows how many deaths Mao was responsible for, directly or indirectly. In the first months after the establishment of the People's Republic, when the Army was consolidating control of the country, there was ample opportunity for individuals to "settle scores," avenge past wrongs. Many landowners were killed. Many intellectuals and city dwellers sentenced to do hard manual work in extreme heat or cold were not strong enough to survive. Some committed suicide. John King Fairbank of Harvard puts the range of "sober estimates" of deaths from 1949 through 1952 at two to five million.

To learn how to convert Communist theory into the modern machinery they needed, the leaders of the Chinese Communist Party turned to the example of the only other large Communist nation, the Soviet Union. Stalin had sought to modernize his nation by concentrating most of his effort and money on heavy industry. The Soviet people's desires for automobiles, sewing machines, even for better housing, would have to wait. First the nation needed steel mills, mining equipment, locomotives, dynamos, modern weapons. Those increased her productive capacity and her military strength. Stalin had set forth his program in a series of Five Year Plans, with specified projects and goals.

In 1953, Mao began his first Five Year Plan for China. It included 1,600 major projects. Production of steel and machine tools was to be tripled; of cement and electric power doubled. The railroads were to be extended into the sparsely populated northwest, and new mines opened there. The Soviet Union sent thousands of technicians to China to assist in the work, and trade between the two nations increased greatly. It seemed China and the Soviet Union would stand together in opposition to the capitalist countries.

But in 1953, Stalin died. Nikita Khrushchev became head of the Communist Party in the Soviet Union, and eventually Stalin's successor as head of state. In 1965, he set as the goal of Soviet foreign policy "peaceful coexistence" with the Western nations, with competition continuing in economic and political areas. Mao believed that war between the Communist and capitalist countries was inevitable. China and the Soviet Union moved further and further apart on questions of international communist policy. In time Mao would feel that China was strong enough to oppose both the United States and the Soviet Union, and use one against the other in a power triangle.

Even in China there was not complete agreement on the right path to the goal of a socialist state, the best way of "building socialism." Mao, with his interest in the people, emphasized equality for all, and training the masses to take part in the processes of government. Other party leaders favored Stalin's path of first developing the economy. The two emphases were called the "mass line" of thought and the "economist line." But the second was also derided as the "revisionist line," because Mao said it revised the original pure doctrine of Marx and Lenin. Intellectuals discussed the two lines and many variations on them. In 1956, Mao invited public discussions of government shortcomings, quoting from the classics the words, "Let a hundred flowers bloom together, let a hundred schools of thought contend." Perhaps he sincerely thought that in free discussion his thought would overcome all disagreement. Perhaps he wanted to gauge the extent of dissatisfaction with what he had done so far. Some have suggested the invitation was a trap. At any rate, Mao was shocked by the quantity of criticism expressed. The Hundred Flowers Campaign came to an abrupt halt.

The first Five Year Plan, with its emphasis on industry, was drawing to a close. For the next five years, beginning in 1958, Mao proposed a strategy of "walking on two legs," to develop both industry (for the economists) and agriculture (for the masses). China would thus achieve a Great Leap Forward. Expansion of heavy industry continued. Mao called on the masses to mobilize for ambitious schemes nationwide. Since steel was always in short supply, a million small furnaces were set up in backyards to smelt iron. Teams worked to expand small industries all across the country, especially those producing farm machinery. Flood control and irrigation work increased the amount of land available for growing food. Other teams gave their attention to land already under cultivation, to increase its yield.

The major tactic for increasing land yield was the introduction of agricultural "communes." The problem produced by the land distribution of 1950—100 million farms each too small for efficient operation—had been met by forming village cooperatives. Families still owned their own farms, but shared in the ownership of machinery, food processing plants and so on. Enthusiasts of the Great Leap Forward believed cooperation could be carried much further. Members of many cooperatives could join together in a commune. There, party leaders would organize all of life for maximum production. To allow women more time to work, community mess halls and child care centers were set up. Production brigades were assigned work to do in various places, twenty-eight days each month. To make this program possible, each family was required to contribute all its land and private possessions, down to pots and pans, to the commune. In return, each person received as much food as the leaders deemed adequate, and other ncessities.

The result of all this organization was a sharp *decrease* in food production. The party leaders often knew little about running a farm. The only incentive for the workers to work hard was the vague objective of "building socialism," and the Chinese land responded best to intensive cultivation by a family that knew and loved every square foot they planted. To make matters worse, bad weather that year and the next decreased crop yield still further. Shortages plagued the country. Food had to be severely rationed. Hungry citizens in every type of work lost their zeal for the Great Leap Forward. And the Central Committee of the party paid a bit more attention when members argued for the economist line.

The most eloquent advocate of that line, surprisingly enough, was a longtime colleague of Mao; the two had worked together organizing socialist youth in 1920. His name was Liu Shaoqi. Liu had risen along with Mao, and was now first vice-chairman of the party. When the Constitution of 1954 was adopted, with a provision for a chairman and a vice-chairman of the republic, Mao and Liu were the two chosen for the posts. After the dismal statistics of the Great Leap Forward began to come in, Mao announced that he would not be a candidate for another term as chairman of the republic. (His term in the more powerful position of chairman of the party still had some years to run.) Liu was chosen for the post.

Liu set about correcting the mistakes of the Great Leap Forward, mistakes which Mao admitted. He was greatly helped by the secretary general of the party, a very short, very practical man named Deng Xiaoping. Deng had also been with Mao from the 1920s, and was one of the veterans of the Long March. But Deng was less interested in abstract political theory than either Mao or Liu. He now proposed that the farmers would produce more food if they were given at least some land for their own again. He said, in a statement still remembered for its ideology and its wit, "Private farming is all right as long as it raises production, just as it doesn't matter whether a cat is black or white as long as it catches mice." Mao was not pleased by Deng's independence. He once growled, "Deng is deaf, yet at meetings he takes a seat far from me." But the remedies of Liu and Deng helped, and the weather improved, and by 1962, conditions were better for the people. Commenting on the part the weather played, Liu said, "The recent disasters were three-tenths natural and seven-tenths manmade." Mao's mass line was questioned more and more.

Mao had an explanation for the problems encountered —and his own solution.

It was now more than a decade since the founding of the People's Republic. State ownership of mills and factories had gradually replaced private ownership, and most posts in the government were now held by members of the Communist Party. The party had grown from 2.7 million members in 1947 to 17 million in 1961. But certain areas of the national life were still dominated by leaders from an earlier day, who were not Communists. Higher education was one such area, perhaps the most troubling one for Mao. University professors had no use for the lessons of political indoctrination the Communists had introduced into every class in the primary schools. Their students needed all their time at the universities for learning science or mathematics or whatever. Mao's answer was the slogan "Better Red than expert." That is to say, right thinking is more important than great knowledge. Perhaps Mao was guided too much by his own experience. His own education had been often interrupted. But he was a deep thinker with a brilliant mind. Not many could follow his example.

The problems of the Great Leap Forward may have been caused, Mao felt, by the nation not being Red enough, not enough committed to communist doctrine. Even some party members were lacking in socialist zeal. When the Agrarian Reform Act of 1950 gave the land of the rich landlords to the farmers, it also gave them the right to sell it. In some villages the Communist cadres, sent to teach the farmers, bought up the small plots, and became landlords themselves. Less enterprising cadres had simply settled down in soft jobs in the government bureaucracy. Their contribution to building socialism was filling out forms and filing reports. Those who rose to positions of some power often used their influence to obtain scarce goods or favors, such as university admission for their children. They were doing nothing to further Mao's goal of equality for all the people. In fact, as the nation's industry grew, inequality grew. The people who worked in factories had always had a higher standard of living than those who worked on farms, and now more and more of the young were migrating to the cities. Not enough responded to Mao's exhortations to lead the hard life of a pioneer in the distant northwest provinces to help develop China's vast untapped natural resources. Liu and Deng were always talking about the need for bonuses and other material incentives to get people to work harder. Nobody worked harder than Mao, except perhaps Zhou Enlai. And Mao lived very simply. The only luxuries he really enjoyed were cigarettes in ample supply, and a huge personal library. The proper incentive for work was the desire "to serve the people." China was losing the fervor of the stirring days of the 1940s. A new revolution was needed, Mao felt, a revolution of minds.

The purest Communist doctrine in China was still to be found, Mao believed, in the ranks of the People's Liberation Army. General Lin Biao, its commander in the Korean War, was now Minister of Defense, and Mao's strong supporter in Central Committee meetings. Another effective ally was Mao's fourth wife, Jiang Qing. Jiang Qing had joined the Party in her early twenties, when she was at the beginning of an acting career. After making several films in Shanghai, she set out on the dangerous trip to the Communist stronghold in Yan'an in 1937. There she sat in the front row for one of Mao's lectures and clapped louder than anyone else to attract his attention. She need not have worried. She was very beautiful, and Mao appreciated that as well as revolutionary zeal.

In late 1965, Mao, Lin and Jiang Qing announced the beginning of a Great Proletarian Cultural Revolution. The first campaign of the Revolution was directed against "Four Olds": old ideas, old culture, old customs, old habits. In May, 1966, the party Central Committee announced: "The representatives of the bourgeoisie who have infiltrated the party, the government and the army are a bunch of counterrevolutionary revisionists." In other words, the new Revolution was directed against the economist line of Chairman of the Republic Liu Shaoqi and Deng Xiaoping. Since it was a Cultural Revolution, its battles were intended to be fought with words, not bullets. Mao gave a wide invitation to all people to "talk, discuss, criticize" the party, the army, their superiors, counterrevolutionaries everywhere.

In 1919, the students in Peking were the prime movers in the May Fourth Movement for a stronger China. In 1966, students again took the lead. Their word-bullets appeared on the walls of Peking University and its neighbor Qinghua University as large-character "posters"—political essays written very large so that a crowd standing round can read them. They demanded more political debate in the universities, and a more liberal admissions policy.

Other young people soon joined the movement—students in high schools, and young factory workers. They quickly organized and called themselves the Red Guards. Liu and Deng sent teams of cadres to try to restrain them, but Mao congratulated the young on their initiative. The young could remember no government of China but his, and he counted on them to provide much of the energy for the new revolution. Two years before, Lin Biao had had published a small volume of quotations from Mao's writings. This "Little Red Book" was soon a sort of badge for the Red Guards, along with a red armband. They traveled all over the country to "exchange experiences," participating in new Long Marches or traveling free on the trains. On August 18, 1966, a million Red Guards passed in review before Mao in Peking. Similar parades were held in other cities. The young marchers carried huge portraits of Mao, and flags and banners. Many beat on drums and gongs. Sometimes the occasion seemed more like a carnival than a political demonstration. When the Red Guards added the students of another school or the workers of another factory to their ranks, they decorated the entrance with purple paper lanterns and a red cloth covered with flowers, and celebrated by shooting off firecrackers half the night.

For a time the country was near chaos. All schools and universities were closed. Factory schedules were disrupted. Some took the challenge "destroy old culture" to mean destroy works of art produced by the old culture, and many great treasures were lost. Jiang Qing, the former actress, took as her special responsibility the remolding of the performing arts. The Peking Opera's glorious repertory of Chinese classics was thrown out, for instance, and replaced by eight new operas with political themes. Music by Beethoven and other composers of the West was banned from China as dangerously capitalistic.

In Shanghai, China's largest city, resistance to the Red Guards was the strongest, because of the very problems Mao had identified. The city's many factories had created a group of relatively well-paid workers, and the municipal government was a huge bureaucracy. A committee for the Cultural Revolution took over the newspapers, however, and soon deposed the mayor. After that, the committee's leaders were to play a prominent part in the national government.

Some Red Guards had as a slogan "Criticize every-

A theatrical version of a river crossing during the Long March, the great saga of Communist China. During the Great Cultural Revolution, Mao's wife, Jiang Qing, saw to it that all the performing arts taught Communist doctrine.

thing." Soon it was not at all clear just what evils the Cultural Revolution sought to correct. But it was completely clear that it supported one individual, Mao Zedong. Mao had once deplored the "cult of personality," any tend-

ency to treat a leader as a god. Now the "cult of Mao" served his purposes. He was often described as the "Great Helmsman," needed to steer China through stormy waters. When it was apparent to all that he could still command enormous forces in China, he directed the Army to restore order. Some units of Red Guards had gotten a taste of power and were reluctant to give it up. In some provinces they seemed almost young versions of the warlords of the 1920s and held deadly pitched battles with each other. But by the end of 1969, order was restored throughout the country.

Liu and Deng were removed from their posts. Deng was sent to work in a mess hall out in the country in order that he might learn more about serving the people. Liu's whereabouts were unknown for a long time, and his death some years later went unannounced. The young people of China had been made aware of political issues, and many party positions were now held by younger members. The universities now had to pay much more attention to politics, admitting students from all ranks of the people, rather than only those able to pass strict exams or whose parents had influence. And once again Mao would emphasize that the working man must play an important role in national life.

In 1969, Mao was seventy-six years old. Lin Biao had been officially designated as his successor. After working so closely with Mao on the Cultural Revolution, it is not surprising that Lin thought he might be ready now for more responsibility. The party was drafting a revised Constitution for China. The draft added another new post at the top, Head of State. As chairman of the party, Mao had been head of state for twenty years without the title. But he saw the dangers of giving one man too much power, if that man was not himself, and he opposed adding the new title to the government. Lin spoke in favor of it, in a speech Mao considered a bid for the job. The two men had already had differences over foreign policy, especially relations with the United States. Mao decided Lin had to go and bit by bit weakened his power. Lin recognized the change in his situation.

Accounts of Lin's end are contradictory. All agree that

in August, 1971, Lin left Peking Airport in a plane heading north. The official Chinese announcement said that he had plotted to kill Mao, the plot was discovered, he fled toward the Soviet Union, the plane crashed in Mongolia and he was killed. The Soviets say they found the plane, but not Lin's body. Some observers of the Chinese scene say the plane was shot down by the Chinese. Others suggest it was shot down by the Soviet Union. Some speculate that Mao eliminated Lin, and invented the story of the plot in order to discredit him. At any rate, Lin was gone, Liu and Deng were removed from power, and now Mao and Zhou Enlai could turn more attention to developments on the international scene.

n 1971, Chiang Kaishek was still in command of the government on Taiwan, which he maintained was the lawful government of all China. He talked less about liberating the mainland from the Communist bandits than he had twenty years before. But he still had his representative in the United Nations. Mao had none. Each year the United Nations considered the question of admitting a representative of the People's Republic. Each year the United States sided with Chiang in opposing the change, and the motion failed, though the vote got closer and closer. The power balance in the world was changing. China was growing stronger. Many of the developing nations in Africa and Asia were looking to her for leadership. She now had her own atomic and hydrogen bombs.

China's position as a model for young nations displeased the leaders of the Soviet Union, who were accustomed to directing Communist party policies worldwide. China's military strength also alarmed them, since the Chinese-Soviet border is more than three thousand miles long. The split between the two countries that had begun

ELEVEN

Reopening Relations with the West

in the 1950s over differences in Communist theory became in the 1960s a dangerous power contest. Both nations increased the number of men and weapons along the border, and occasional incidents of fighting occurred. More important, both nations began to wonder if they were wrong to consider the United States the chief enemy. The struggle between Communist and non-Communist nations was two-sided. Now a three-sided struggle was possible—a power triangle consisting of the Soviet Union, the United States and China.

While China had grown stronger, the United States now had a weaker position in the world, largely because of her involvement in a war in China's neighboring country, Vietnam. After the Vietnamese drove the French out of their country in 1954, they were unable to agree on conditions for an election of a national government. As had happened in Korea, the Communists in the north fought with the anti-Communists in the south for control. In the 1960s, military strategists in the United States became convinced that this war threatened American interests in the Pacific. American arms and advisers returned to Vietnam,

*Premier Zhou Enlai is greeted by Chairman Mao on his
return from a 1964 trip to Moscow. Zhou, Mao's right hand
man for forty-eight years, and his country's champion
at diplomatic negotiations, created over the years a three-way
balance of power for the U.S.S.R., the U.S. and China.*

to be followed in time by fighting men. This involvement
was criticized by many nations, who saw no reason for the
United States to "interfere." As the war continued year after
year with little evidence of progress being made against the
Communists, it was also criticized by many people in the
United States. Dissension over the war grew so serious that

in 1968, President Lyndon Johnson decided not to seek another term in office. His successor, President Richard Nixon, made it his first priority to end the war in Vietnam.

Mao had been aiding the Vietnamese Communists with arms and money for years. He and Zhou Enlai were very interested in the words of the new American president. Zhou had been a chief architect of the 1954 agreement, reached in talks in Geneva, that got the French out of Vietnam. If he could help the United States get out now, he would remove a military threat on China's border, and lessen tensions between the United States and China. That would strengthen China's position versus the Soviet Union. So the very month of the American presidential election, he proposed renewed peace talks on Vietnam. Thinking in Washington proceeded along similar lines. The United States could oppose the Soviet Union with more military strength if the drain of the Vietnam War were stopped. And any step toward better relations between the United States and China would act as a restraint on the actions of the Soviet Union. The Nixon administration lifted long-standing restrictions on trade with the People's Republic, and on travel there by U.S. citizens.

In April, 1971, a group of Americans were in Japan for the World Table Tennis Championships. The Chinese Ping-Pong team won the tournament that year, as they often had in the past. (The Chinese love the sport.) But the Americans, though outclassed, enjoyed playing against the champions, whom they found a friendly group. They were not prepared, however, for what happened next. The Chinese delivered a formal invitation to the American team to visit China the following week. After top level consultations with Washington, the team accepted. And so it was that a group of eighteen—five men and three women players (the youngest a girl of fifteen), plus officers of the United States Table Tennis Association, wives, and three reporters—became the first United States citizens to visit Peking in two decades. The Chinese called it "people's diplomacy." After so many years of bitter attacks by each country on the other, it was important to let ordinary people

Members of the Chinese Ping-Pong team meet a famous American at Disneyland. An exchange of visits by the U.S. and Chinese teams signaled the desire of both nations to work for more friendly relations.

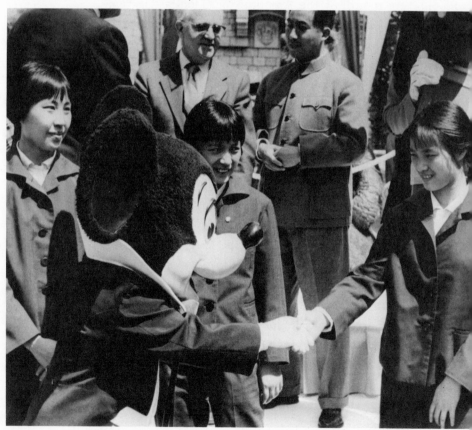

get to know each other in a nonpolitical setting. "Ping Pong diplomacy" the press called it. The Chinese gave the Americans a warm welcome at both the governmental and people levels. They were offered Chinese meals of many courses in both Peking and Shanghai. They visited Qinghua University, scene of the first stirrings of the Cultural Revolution five years before, and played informal matches with the students. They asked to see the Great Wall of China, and the request was granted. They saw two samples of the new theater—the opera *Taking Tiger Mountain by Strategy* and the ballet *The Red Detachment of Women,* both dramatizations of Communism triumphant. Zhou Enlai honored them by receiving them in the Great Hall of the People in Peking, and chatting for nearly two hours. "We have opened a new page in the relations of the Chinese and American people," he told them. In an exhibition table tennis match, the Chinese men's team won 5-3, and the Chinese women's team 5-4. (Later the Chinese team visited the United States.)

At the same time, Mao and Zhou announced that they would welcome a visit from a member of the United States government. President Nixon liked that idea, but wanted to know more about real Chinese intentions before he announced any major steps. Henry Kissinger, his National Security Adviser and later Secretary of State, was the best man to get that information, but sending a top official to China was a major step itself. Consequently, Kissinger, who traveled constantly, included Pakistan on a trip in July, 1971. One morning it was announced to reporters that he was ill and would have to cancel his schedule for the next few days to rest and recover. Actually, Kissinger had departed secretly for Peking. In several days of talks he arranged for President Nixon to visit Peking in February, 1972, to discuss matters of common concern.

*In February 1972, President Richard M. Nixon and National
Security Adviser Henry Kissinger meet with Chairman Mao,
Premier Zhou and an interpreter in Mao's book-lined study.*

In October, 1971, when the annual motion to admit
the People's Republic to the United Nations was presented,
the United States for the first time did not join Chiang
Kaishek's representatives in opposing it. The motion carried,
and Mao's representatives arrived the next month to take
their seats. Chiang and Mao had both maintained since
1949 that China was still a single nation, with only one
legitimate government. Consequently, Chiang's representatives were expelled from the United Nations. Many nations
had already moved their diplomats from Taibei to Peking—
had "granted diplomatic recognition to the People's Republic," in the language of governments. Now many more
did the same. Chiang still had many supporters in the
United States, however, so the Nixon administration continued—officially—to recognize his government.

    That was the most difficult problem the President had
to deal with in the talks in Peking the following February.
He arrived in China with Henry Kissinger and a large group
of other advisers, plus a team of reporters and television
cameramen. Although heads of state who visit other countries are customarily entertained at lavish banquets, few
countries can prepare such lavish banquets as the Chinese.
Zhou Enlai was the host at the banquet in the Great Hall
of the People that opened the visit. Mao was saving his
limited strength—he was now seventy-eight years old—for
serious talks in private. An orchestra played all during the
evening. In honor of the guests, they had learned "America
the Beautiful," and played it over and over: "Oh beautiful
for spacious skies, for amber waves of grain." President
Nixon complimented Premier Zhou on the music. "That
was the music they played at your inaugural," Zhou replied. "I thought you would like it for tonight." Thanks to
television transmission by space satellite, viewers in the

United States could see, live, the endless toasts and smiles that were exchanged that night. The Americans might have called their answer to "people's diplomacy" "media diplomacy." By the end of the visit, many telecasts later, there were few Americans who did not know that relations with China had changed.

Away from the cameras, smiles were fewer. Yes, both countries desired better relations, more trade, more exchanges of people. Yes, both countries wanted to end the war in Vietnam. But what was to be done about that government on Taiwan? Chairman Mao wanted diplomatic recognition for the People's Republic, but that was politically unpopular in the United States. It required more preparation of American voters. President Nixon wanted a signed guarantee that Mao would not take Taiwan by force, but for Mao such a guarantee would be an admission that there were really "two Chinas." It was obvious that there had been two Chinas since 1949, but Mao (and Chiang) had been denying it too long to change now. In the end the diplomats worked out a statement that the two governments could issue at the close of the talks. Along with expressing many hopes for improved relations, it said that the United States "does not challenge" the position that Taiwan is a part of China. In order not to give the statement too much significance in the eyes of the world, it was not issued in Peking, but in Shanghai where the

President Nixon, Jiang Qing (Mao's wife) and Mrs. Nixon applaud a performance of Chinese ballet. In Mao's last years, his wife led a powerful group in the government known as the Gang of Four.

Americans stopped on their way home, and was called simply the Shanghai Communique.

The Nixon trip, inconclusive as it was, was the high point in relations between the two countries for some years to come. It did lead to an increase in exchanges of scientists, performing arts groups and athletes. But soon after the President got home, his administration was shaken by a scandal known as Watergate. And in Peking more and more attention was going to the question of who would be Chairman Mao's successor.

Over the years, Mao had turned against two men who seemed likely candidates. Liu Shaoqi, made Chairman of the Republic in 1958, had turned out to be too much of a revisionist. General Lin Biao had seemed too eager to get too much power in his own hands. Premier Zhou Enlai, who had made the greatest contribution to China's development after Mao himself, was only four years younger than Mao, and his health was failing. It appears that Mao and Zhou decided that, after Mao, China should be governed by a group. Zhou began to assemble members of the group. An agricultural expert named Hua Guofeng had attracted Mao's attention by his work in the party in Mao's native province of Hunan. Zhou had brought him to Peking in 1971, and in 1973 he was elected to the Politburo of the Central Committee. In 1975 he was named one of the twelve vice-premiers. Zhou had long admired the organizing skills of a man he had known since they were young Communists together in France—Deng Xiaoping. Despite Mao's frequent differences with Deng, and his dismissal in the Cultural Revolution, Zhou brought the tough little survivor back into the government, and it was clear Zhou favored him as his own successor. Hua and Deng were good administrators who were more interested in getting a job done than in the political theory that went with it. At Central Committee meetings, politics was often expounded by Mao's wife, Jiang Qing. Her work during the Cultural Revolution had substituted politics for art throughout China. It was clear she wanted at least the post in the cabinet of Minister of Culture, and some believed she hoped to be Mao's successor herself. Comparisons, not always complimentary, were made between her and the Dowager Empress Ci Xi who had dominated China for so long. In 1972, Jiang Qing, twenty-one years Mao's junior, was fifty-seven years old. They had been married thirty-three years. Working closely with her was a handsome man still in his thirties, Wang Hongwen. He had risen to prominence as an organizer of the Red Guards in Shanghai—risen so rapidly that he (with others like him) was called a "helicopter." In 1973, he was named to the Politburo and made a vice-chairman, in the number three place just after Mao and Zhou. Two other men from Shanghai, both journalists before the Cultural Revolution, were now members of the Politburo: Zhang Chungqiao, whose position as Chairman of the Shanghai Revolutionary Committee had made him, in effect, mayor of the city, and Yao Wenyuan, who had been in charge of propaganda. Wang, Zhang and Yao often voted with Jiang Qing in meetings, and that group was in time named the "Gang of Four."

Mao watched all the leading contenders closely. One day he offered some concise advice to three of them, plus his ever-faithful Zhou Enlai: "Zhou should rest more. Deng should work more. Wang should study more. Jiang Qing should talk less." Like many husbands, he often complained about his wife's talkativeness. She should take a tip from nature, he said. "The ears are made to remain open, but the mouth may shut."

Outside observers studied the promotions, even compared photos taken at state dinners to see who sat closest to Mao, or Zhou, in an effort to guess who Mao's successor would be. Deng Xiaoping was clearly the one with the longest experience. He also had an inner strength built up in his years of near exile. But he was only ten years younger than Mao, and Mao wanted more young blood in the government. Deng was not his favorite candidate. There was not much time left.

In 1974, Zhou Enlai's health worsened, and he had to spend months in the hospital. During that time, Deng managed the day-to-day running of the government, in consultation with Zhou. Mao still received visiting heads of state, impressed them with his grasp of world affairs, and worked to make them friends of the People's Republic. But he did not have the stamina for long hours of political discussion. In December, 1974, the National People's Congress, the nearly powerless legislative body, met secretly in Peking. Zhou left the hospital to preside; Mao did not attend. After the Congress a new roster of officials was announced. Zhou was still Premier, but now Deng was one of six Vice-Chairmen of the Party, and First Vice-Premier. Whoever might succeed Mao, Deng would succeed Zhou, the China watchers said. The Congress also approved a new, shorter Constitution to replace the one adopted in 1954. It seemed to be a compromise document, with some provisions reflecting the economist line and some the mass line. It spoke of a "permanent revolution," and guaranteed workers "freedom to strike." But it also guaranteed farmers the right to maintain the private plots that Mao had often tried to abolish. It guaranteed "freedom of speech, correspondence, the press, assembly, association, procession and demonstration." It also granted freedom of worship to those who want it, and freedom to propagate atheism to those who want that. While constitutional guarantees are of little value in a nation where one man has supreme power, the new Constitution did seem to reflect a desire for more stable and orderly government in the years ahead.

On April 5, 1975, Chiang Kaishek, eighty-eight years old, died on Taiwan. His son Chiang Chingkuo succeeded him as President.

In 1976, the time came to resolve many questions. On January 8, Zhou's long illness reached its end. It is reported that he said to the hospital personnel attending him, "Nothing to do here. Go look after other sick comrades. They need you more." And then he was gone. It was his desire that no monumental mausoleum be built for him, and to make sure of that, he directed that his body be cremated. His widow carried out his wishes in the matter. The people's grief at news of his death made it clear he was greatly beloved in China, and around the world statesmen spoke of his strength, skill and moderation.

Zhou had had many clashes with Jiang Qing and her allies, usually because he found their proposals too extreme. Now they were able to block the naming of Deng as premier. As a compromise, Hua Guofeng, the administrator, was chosen. When a crowd of 100,000 gathered in Peking in April to honor Zhou's memory, the ceremony was canceled, and a riot ensued. The Central Committee said Deng was responsible for the riot, and removed him from the government again.

July, 1976, brought two more important events. Gen-

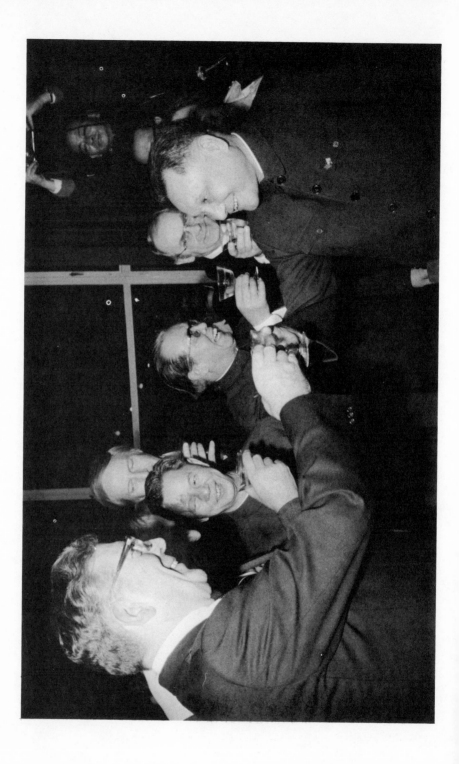

eral Zhu De, Mao's partner in the battles against Chiang Kaishek back in the 1930s, died at the age of eighty-nine. And before dawn on July 28, the worst earthquake recorded anywhere in the world in a dozen years hit the industrial city of Tangshan a hundred miles east of Peking. Tangshan had a population of a million. It is estimated that 655,000 were killed in the city and surrounding areas, as 117 buildings collapsed completely, seven speeding trains were derailed, and factory machinery going full tilt was shaken to pieces. Ten thousand were killed just in one locomotive works. As the earth opened in places, whole houses dropped into underground caverns. Pressure under the surface caused by the quake sent geysers of sand spouting ten feet into the air, burying farms. The government organized disaster relief and rebuilding operations quickly and effectively, and declined offers of help from other countries. Because of the possibility that another quake might hit Peking itself, millions of people were moved out of their apartments to live in tents for the summer.

The Emperor Kang Xi would have drawn a very clear conclusion from such a natural disaster: the dynasty had lost the mandate of heaven. It was time for a new dynasty to take its place. Mao didn't believe anything like that about earthquakes. There was no provision in the government for him to resign in favor of someone else. Only death could end his rule. On September 9, 1976, it did.

Vice Premier Deng Xiaoping and Leonard Woodcock, Chief of the U.S. Liaison Office in Peking, drink a toast on January 1, 1979, the day their two countries resumed normal diplomatic relations.

After the funeral was over and eloquent praises of Mao from all over the world stopped coming in, the Politburo would raise Hua Guofeng from Premier to Chairman of the Party, would put Jiang Qing and the Gang of Four under arrest, and restore Deng Xiaoping to his post of Vice-Premier. Deng and Hua would begin a new campaign to modernize China in agriculture, industry, science and technology and defense by the year 2000, with the help of

After Mao Zedong's death on September 9, 1976, thousands of Chinese of every sort came to pay their last respects. His body lay in state in Peking's Tiananmen Square, in the Great Hall of the People.

many Western nations. In December, 1978, Deng and United States President Jimmy Carter would announce that China and the United States were resuming normal diplomatic relations. The rule of Mao was over.

Yet it is not too much to say, as many did at the time of his death, that after Mao the world will never be the same. Mao's leadership developed weak China into a dominant factor in world affairs. Her military strength cannot be ignored. Her expanding economy makes her an important trading partner for many nations. Mao insisted that the people are the source of a nation's strength, and that the

people, properly led and motivated, can overcome all obstacles and provide for themselves a good society. By Western standards his methods were harsh and ruthless, and what he called motivation amounted to coercion and thought control. (His most ardent admirers ask that these matters be judged not by Western standards, but by the Chinese ones of the 2000 years before him.) But what was remarkable was not how many people Mao coerced, but how many responded gladly to his call to "serve the people." There can be no denying that the People's Republic he created has made good progress in expanding education for all children and in improving housing. And it has succeeded in providing adequate food and clothing and basic medical care for a nation of nearly a billion people. Of greatest significance in the long run will be the example China offers for the political development of other countries—both those already in the Communist group and those that have recently gained independence from foreign domination. They are well aware of the truth of Mao's words on October 1, 1949: "The Chinese people have stood up."

Bibliography

Bagrow, Leo. *History of Cartography* (trans. D. L. Paisey) Cambridge, Mass.: Harvard University Press, 1964

Bloodworth, Dennis. *The Chinese Looking Glass*. New York: Farrar, Straus, and Giroux, 1967

Boorman, Howard L., ed. *Biographical Dictionary of Republican China*, Vol. I. New York: Columbia University Press, 1967

Cameron, Nigel. *Peking*. New York: Harper and Row, 1967

Chen, Jerome. *Mao and the Chinese Revolution*. London: Oxford University Press, 1965

Chesneaux, Jean et al. (trans. Paul Auster and Lydia Davis). *China: The People's Republic, 1949–1976*. New York: Pantheon, 1979

Clubb, O. Edmund. *Twentieth Century China*. New York: Columbia University Press, 1963

Eberhard, Wolfram. *A History of China from the Earliest Times to the Present Day*. Berkeley/Los Angeles: University of California Press, 1969

The Editors of Time. *Ancient China*. New York: Time-Life Books, 1967

Elegant, Robert. *The Center of the World*, 2nd Edit. New York: Funk & Wagnalls, 1967

Fairbank, John K. *The United States and China*, 4th ed. Cambridge, Mass.: Harvard University Press, 1979

Fairbank, John K., Reischauer, Edwin O. and Craig, Albert M. *East Asia: The Modern Transformation.* Boston: Houghton Mifflin, 1965

Fitzgerald, C. P. *The Birth of Communist China.* London: Penguin, 1964

Fitzgerald, C. P. *The Horizon History of China.* New York: American Heritage Publishing Co., 1969

Fleming, Peter. *The Siege at Peking.* New York: Harper, 1959

Giles, Herbert A. *A Chinese Biographical Dictionary.* Taipei: Literature House, 1962

Goodrich, Luther Carrington. *A Short History of the Chinese People*, 3rd ed. New York: Harper, 1959

Hahn, Emily. *Chiang Kai-shek, an unauthorized biography.* N.Y.: Doubleday, 1955

Harrison, John A. *China Since 1800.* New York: Harbinger (Harcourt, Brace, and World Paper), 1967

Hsu, Immanuel C. Y. *The Rise of Modern China.* New York: Oxford University Press, 1970

Hummel, Arthur W. (ed.). *Eminent Chinese of the Ch'ing Period.* Washington: U.S. Library of Congress, 1943

Isaacs, Harold R. *The Tragedy of the Chinese Revolution*, rev. ed. Stanford: Stanford University Press, 1961

Latourette, Kenneth Scott. *The Development of China.* New York: Houghton Mifflin, 1946

Malraux, Andre. *Anti-Memoires.* New York: Holt, Rinehart, and Winston, 1968

Mathews, R. H. *A Chinese-English Dictionary* (Wade-Giles), rev. American ed. Cambridge: Harvard University Press, 1950

Michael, Franz. *The Taiping Rebellion, History and Documents.* Seattle: University of Washington Press, 1966

National Geographic Society. *Atlas of the World.* Washington, D.C.: 1963

Pelissier, Roger (trans. Martin Kieffer). *The Awakening of China, 1793–1949.* New York: Putnam, 1967

Purcell, Victor. *The Boxer Uprising, A Background Study.* Cambridge: Cambridge University Press, 1963

Rostow, Walt Whitman, et al. *The Prospects for Communist China.* Cambridge, Mass: Massachusetts Institute of Technology Press, 1954

Ryckmans, Pierre (writing under the pseudonym Simon Leys). *Chinese Shadows.* New York: Penguin, 1978

Schurman, Franz and Schell, Orville, ed. *The China Reader,* Vols. I & II. New York: Random House, 1967

Scott, John. *China, the Hungry Dragon.* New York: Parents Magazine Press, 1967

Snow, Edgar. *Red Star Over China,* rev. ed. New York: Grove Press, 1968

Spence, Jonathan. *Ts'ao Yin and the K'ang Hsi Emperor; Bondservant and Master.* New Haven: Yale University Press, 1966

Tan, Chester. *The Boxer Catastrophe.* New York: Columbia University Press, 1955

Teng, Ssu-yu and Fairbank, John K. *China's Response to the West . . . 1839–1923.* New York: Atheneum, 1963

Terrill, Ross. *The Future of China After Mao.* New York: Delacorte Press, 1978

Tuchman, Barbara. *Stilwell and the American Experience in China.* New York: Macmillan, 1971

United States Department of State. *The United States' Relations with China.* Washington, D.C.: Government Printing Office, 1949

White, Theodore H. and Jacoby, Annalee. *Thunder Out of China*. New York: William Sloane Associates, 1946

Wu, C. K., Wu, K. S. et al. *Chinese to English Dictionary* (Pinyin system of romanization). Monterey, Ca.: Chinese Language Research Assoc., 1976

Index